Exceptional Cars
Alfa Romeo T33/TT/3

Porter Press International

Also published by Porter Press International

Ultimate Series
John Fitzpatrick Group C Porsches – The Definitive History
Works 956 Porsches – The Definitive History
McLaren F1 GTR – The Definitive History
Ferrari 250 GTO – The Definitive History

Great Cars Series
No. 1 – Jaguar Lightweight E-type – The autobiography of 4 WPD
No. 2 – Porsche 917 – The autobiography of 917-023
No. 3 – Jaguar D-type – The autobiography of XKD 504
No. 4 – Ferrari 250 GT SWB – The autobiography of 2119 GT
No. 5 – Maserati 250F – The autobiography of 2528
No. 6 – ERA – The autobiography of R4D
No. 7 – Ferrari 250 GTO – The autobiography of 4153 GT
No. 8 – Jaguar Lightweight E-type – The autobiography of 49 FXN
No. 9 – Jaguar C-type – The autobiography of XKC 051
No. 10 – Lotus 18 – The autobiography of Stirling Moss's '912'
No. 11 – Ford GT40 – The autobiography of 1075
No. 12 – Alfa Romeo Monza – The autobiography of the celebrated 2211130
No. 13 – Bugatti Type 50 – The autobiography of Bugatti's first Le Mans car
No.14 – Shelby Daytona Cobra – The autobiography of CSX2300

Exceptional Cars Series
No. 1 – Iso Bizzarrini – The remarkable history of A3/C 0222
No. 2 – Jaguar XK120 – The remarkable history of JWK 651
No. 3 – Ford GT40 MkII – The remarkable history of 1016
No. 4 – The First Three Shelby Cobras
No. 5 – Aston Martin Ulster – The remarkable history of CMC 614
No. 6 – Maserati 4CLT – The remarkable history of chassis no. 1600
No. 7 – Ferrari 250 LM – The remarkable history of 6313
No. 8 – Ferrari 250 GT SWB – The remarkable history of 2689
No. 9 – Ferrari 857S – The remarkable history of 0578M

Porter Profiles
No. 1 – Austin Healey – The story of DD 300
No. 2 – Jaguar D-type – The story of XKD 526

Bespoke books
The Le Mans Model Collection 1949-2009 (three-book set)
Derek Bell – All my Porsche races
DB4 G.T. Continuation – History in the making
One Formula, 50 years of car design – Gordon Murray
The Self Preservation Society – 50 Years of The Italian Job
The All-American Hero and Jaguar's Racing E-types
JUE 477 – The Remarkable History & Restoration of the World's First Production Land-Rover
ROFGO Collection
The Light Car Company Rocket
Ferrari 250 GTE

Scrapbooks
Stirling Moss Scrapbook 1929-1954
Stirling Moss Scrapbook 1955
Stirling Moss Scrapbook 1956-1960
Stirling Moss Scrapbook 1961
Graham Hill Scrapbook 1929-1966
Murray Walker Scrapbook
Martin Brundle Scrapbook
Barry Cryer Comedy Scrapbook
Mini Scrapbook

The Jaguar Portfolio
Ultimate E-type – The Competition Cars
Jaguar E-type – The Definitive History (2nd edition)
Original Jaguar XK (3rd edition)
Jaguar Design – A Story of Style
Saving Jaguar

Deluxe leather-bound, signed, limited editions with slipcases are available for many titles. Books available from retailers or signed copies (of most titles) direct from the publishers. To order, simply phone +44 (0)1584 781588, visit the website or email sales@porterpress.co.uk

Keep up-to-date with news about current books and new releases at: **www.porterpress.co.uk**

Exceptional Cars

Alfa Romeo T33/TT/3

The remarkable story of 115.72.002

Ian Wagstaff

Porter Press International

© Porter Press International

All rights reserved. No part of this publication may be reproduced, stored in a retrieval system or transmitted, in any form or by any means, electronic, mechanical, photocopying, recording or otherwise, without prior permission in writing from the publisher

First published in September 2020

978-1-907085-34-5

Published by
Porter Press International

Hilltop Farm, Knighton-on-Teme, Tenbury Wells, WR15 9LY, UK
Tel: +44 (0)1584 781588
sales@porterpress.co.uk
www.porterpress.co.uk

Edited by Steve Rendle
Design & Layout by Martin Port

Printed by Gomer Press Ltd

COPYRIGHT

We have made every effort to trace and acknowledge copyright holders and we apologise in advance for any unintentional omission. We would be pleased to insert the appropriate acknowledgement in any subsequent edition.

Contents

Introduction 6

Part 1 Back on the world stage 8

1   Alfa Romeo heritage 10
2   Birth of the Tipo 33 16
3   Enter the T33/TT/3 22

Part 2 The factory car 28

4   The Americas 30
5   To Europe 42
6   The Alfas race on 64

Part 3 On three continents 70

7   Greek Odyssey 72
8   Home and abroad 82
9   Return to Sicily 92
10 A part of history 100
11 Photo gallery 108

Acknowledgements & bibliography 126

Index 127

Introduction

It was one of the finest laps ever witnessed on Sicily's 72km (45-mile) Piccolo Circuit. The pride of Alfa Romeo was at stake and an inspired, possessed even, Helmut Marko had given his all.

Alfa had dominated that classic of road racing, the Targa Florio, throughout the early 1930s, with six consecutive wins, but the pickings from then on had been slim, and with the exception of a single victory in 1950, the Milanese team would not win in Sicily again until 1971 when local hero Nino Vaccarella and Dutchman Toine Hezemans spearheaded a resounding victory. Having re-established a toehold on the summit, Alfa Romeo wanted to stay there and, in 1972, entered four cars. Ferrari, which up until that point in the season had regularly beaten the Alfas, had shown little interest and just sent what might best be described as a single-car reserve team. The 1972 Targa Florio was Alfa Romeo's to lose.

The problem was, that with three laps to go, the Alfa effort seemed to be falling apart and that lone Ferrari had a lead of nearly two minutes. What followed has been described as perhaps Marko's greatest drive. He threw the Alfa around the tight circuit, past spectators dangerously lining the road, through both countryside and the unforgiving buildings of towns and villages. The Ferrari finished first on the road – cars were sent off individually on the Targa Florio and raced against the clock – and a tense crowd waited for the Alfa to arrive at the finish line. When it did, it was still 17 seconds adrift. Marko had failed to retain the Targa for Alfa Romeo, but what a magnificent failure.

The car that Helmut Marko drove that day was an Alfa Romeo T33/TT/3, one of the tubular-framed developments of the Tipo 33 concept that the factory team, Autodelta, raced for just one season. Specifically, it was chassis number 115.72.002.

Three years later, Autodelta boss Carlo Chiti would sell what he said was this very car to Greek racing driver George Moschous and it would experience a perhaps unique life in Greece, away from the eyes of mainstream motorsport. Preserved in almost original condition, it would go on to become an important historic racer, first travelling to compete in Japan and South Africa while in the custody of its next owners, Andrew Fletcher and Willie Tuckett, and then becoming a regular at European events, first in the hands of Franco Meiners and then with its current owner, Martin Halusa. It would also relive its Targa Florio glory as the star of a Red Bull promotional video, driven by current Formula 1 driver, Daniel Ricciardo.

This is the story of that car.

Ian Wagstaff
Chinnor, England
June 2020

● Alfa Romeo T33/TT/3 chassis number 115.72.002's finest hour came on 21 May 1972, when Helmut Marko hurled the V8 car round the Sicilian roads that he thoroughly disliked in a heroic attempt to catch Arturo Merzario's Ferrari 312PB.
www.motoprint.co.za

Part 1
Back on the world stage

Once the star of international motorsport, Alfa Romeo's light had waned by the late 1960s. There had been times during the inter-war period that it had shone supreme in grand prix and endurance racing, and even when the Teutonic might of Mercedes-Benz and Auto Union usurped it, the incomparable Tazio Nuvolari still took an Alfa Romeo to victory in the Silver Arrows' back yard. In the immediate post-World War II period, there were no cars that could match the supercharged Alfa Romeo Tipo 158 and 159, with the first two official Formula 1 World Championships falling to its drivers. However, by the end of 1951 the light was beginning to fade, Ferrari was now rising in the firmament, and Alfa Romeo withdrew from top-line international racing.

In the 1930s, what would later become known as sportscar racing had been the preserve of Alfa Romeo. In the leading endurance contests of its native Italy – the Mille Miglia and the Targa Florio – it reigned with an imperial might. Four consecutive Le Mans 24 Hours races fell to its legendary type 8C.

It was therefore perhaps not surprising that when Alfa Romeo decided to return to international competition for 1967 it chose to develop a line of sports prototypes. Known as the Tipo 33s, these cars developed to a point where, in 1971, they were fast enough to win three rounds of the International Championship for Makes, including, once more, the Targa Florio. The following year's evolution would be the T33/TT/3.

Chassis 115.72.002 would be the most celebrated.

● The first sight of an Alfa Romeo T33/TT/3 in public was in practice for the 1971 Targa Florio, where it is seen here being driven by German, Rolf Stommelen. *Alamy*

Chapter 1
Alfa Romeo Heritage

As A.L.F.A ([Società] Anonima Lombarda Fabbrica Automobili), Alfa Romeo had participated in its first Targa Florio prior to World War I. Taken over by entrepreneur Nicola Romeo's operation during that conflict, the company temporarily ceased production of cars to concentrate on the war effort. After the cessation of hostilities, the company returned to car production, becoming Alfa Romeo in 1920 and setting about creating a sporting legend, attracting the great designer Vittorio Jano away from Fiat, which was then the leading grand prix contender.

The company's first post-war grand prix car – the P.1 – had been handicapped by an engine that failed to produce sufficient power and had been shelved. Jano, though, immediately put the marque into the winner's circle with his supercharged, straight-eight P.2. Antonio Ascari (father of future double Formula 1 World Champion Alberto) had already taken a P.2 to victory in the 1924 Cremona Grand Prix, when three of the cars were entered for the French Grand Prix at Lyons, described by historian David Hodges as 'the supreme race of an era long known as "The Golden Age of Racing"'. It was Alfa's debut at this level, with cars driven by Ascari, burly Giuseppe Campari and the veteran Louis Wagner – an impressive line-up. Campari and Ascari both led, although it was the former who won after his team-mate's engine block cracked. Ascari went on to lead an Alfa 1–2–3–4 victory at the Italian Grand Prix.

The following season underlined 'new boy' Alfa's pre-eminence, with first and second places in both the Belgian and Italian Grands Prix, the first of these headed by Ascari, the second by Gaston Brilli-Peri. Tragically, Ascari was killed leading the 1925 French Grand Prix, resulting in Alfa's withdrawal from the race. A change to the regulations led to the P.2's demotion to non-championship races but, with an increasing number of grands prix being run as Formule Libre events, there were more victories, culminating in Achille Varzi's single-handed win at the 1930 Targa Florio.

Jano returned Alfa to the front rank with the straight-eight P.3, or Tipo B Monoposto, the first genuine single-seater to appear in grand prix racing. Like the P.2, it won first time out, Nuvolari taking the 1932 Italian Grand Prix. Another four major races fell to it that season – the French, German and Monaco Grands Prix and the Targa Florio. The factory Alfa Romeo team withdrew from racing the following year, leaving a former driver, one Enzo Ferrari, to represent it with older 8C models. These were defeated so frequently that Alfa was persuaded to hand the P.3s over to Ferrari, who promptly won six of the season's final 11 events.

Deutschmarks then took over grand prix racing with the might of Mercedes-Benz and Auto Union and the P.3 became obsolescent, although nobody seems to have told Nuvolari when, against all the odds, he defeated all the German cars at the Nürburgring in 1935. It was one of the greatest motorsport victories of all time, underlining both Alfa's and its P.3's place in motorsport legend.

- Le Mans became Alfa Romeo's playground in the early 1930s. In 1932 the only question seemed to be which of the seven Alfas would be in the lead. In the end it was Raymond Sommer, who won virtually single-handed in his 2.3-litre 8C, his co-driver Luigi Chinetti having been taken ill after just three hours at the wheel. *Motorsport Images*

- Giuseppe Campari won the eventful 1924 French Grand Prix with an Alfa Romeo P.2. His team-mate, Antonio Ascari, retired his car after 34 laps with a cracked block. His mechanic, Giulio Ramponi, is seen here trying in vain to push-start the car down the slight gradient past the pits. *Motorsport Images*

Alfa Romeo Heritage

- In 1935, Tazio Nuvolari, driving a Scuderia Ferrari-entered Alfa Romeo Tipo B, stunned the normally dominant Mercedes-Benz and Auto Union teams by beating them on home soil. The little Italian's victory in the German Grand Prix that day has gone down as one of the greatest in motorsport history. *Motorsport Images*

The Italian manufacturers, though, began to despair of ever again being able to take on the German might. They started to concentrate increasingly on the 1.5-litre voiturette class. This was very much a 'division two' to the grand prix category. However, there was a promise from the rule makers that a 1.5-litre grand prix formula would take effect in 1941. In 1939, the Italian national motorsport federation restricted races in the country to this formula. Designer Gioacchino Colombo, accordingly, created one of the greatest cars in the Alfa Romeo pantheon, the 158 'Alfetta'. During 1939 these were beaten just once, when Mercedes-Benz turned up at Tripoli with two specially built 1.5-litre cars of its own.

Post-war, grand prix racing was categorised as Formula 1 from the 1946 Turin Grand Prix, and the 'Alfettas' dominated the 1947 and 1948 seasons. Alfa did not race in 1949 (mainly

Alfa Romeo Heritage

- Alfa Romeo dominated the first two years of the World Drivers' Championship with its 1.5-litre Tipo 159, a development of the Tipo 158, first introduced before World War II. *Ken Gregory archive*

- The Alfa Romeo 6C, which took three Mille Miglia victories, has been described as a masterpiece of design. Here, Reggie Outlaw takes an example past the shops during the 1930 Tourist Trophy at Ards. He completed nine laps before engine failure. *Motorsport Images*

due to cost, but also the deaths of its drivers Jean-Pierre Wimille and Count Felice Trossi, both of whom died in circumstances unconnected to their racing for Alfa), but returned to contest the new World Championship in 1950, initially with the 158 and then with the updated 159 for 1951. The cars totally dominated that first year, with Giuseppe Farina taking the drivers' title. Alfa had to face a stronger challenge from Ferrari in 1951, but again the title fell to the Milanese team, this time with Juan Manuel Fangio. Alfa Romeo then retired from Formula 1, unable to extract any more from its 158/159s. It was not to be seen again as a constructor in a Formula 1 World Championship race until 1979 (though several teams used Alfa Romeo engines in the intervening years), but half way through the 20th century, it was still perceived as one of the world's most successful manufacturers of racing cars.

During the inter-war period, Alfa Romeo had also become a front-runner in endurance racing, winning every Le Mans 24 Hours race from 1931 to 1934, plus the

Alfa Romeo Heritage

1923 Targa Florio and then six consecutive runnings of the Sicilian contest from 1930 to 1935. All but one of the Mille Miglias that took place from 1928 to 1938 also fell to the marque – some victories taken using what would now be described as genuine sportscars, and others by grand prix cars with two-seater bodies. Alfa's drivers for these long-distance events include memorable names such as Nuvolari, Campari, Varzi, Baconin Borzacchini, Antonio Brivio, Clemente Biondetti, Sir Henry Birkin and Raymond Sommer. The Alfa Romeo 8C, powered by Jano's eight-cylinder engine, first appeared in the early 1930s, becoming one of the most successful endurance racers of all, with four Le Mans victories, three Targa Florios and six Mille Miglias to its name. The earlier 6C, revered as a masterpiece with its silky smooth six-cylinder engine (also designed by Jano), was responsible for three Mille Miglia victories.

There were a few more victories immediately after World War II, with Clemente Biondetti taking the 1947 Mille Miglia in an 8C 2900 B Berlinetta Touring. Three years later, Mario and Giancarlo Bornigia won the Targa Florio with an Alfa Romeo 6C 2500 Competizione. Following its withdrawal from the grand prix scene after the 1951 season, the competition department was given a stay of execution with the C52 'Disco Volante' sportscar, but there was to be no return to glory. A 6C 3000 coupé was, though, driven to second place in the 1953 Mille Miglia by Fangio, a spider version winning the first Supercortemaggiore Grand Prix that year with the same driver. With the failure of the Disco Volante, Alfa again quit the scene.

When the company chose to return to international motor racing for the 1966 season, it was the sportscar discipline, rather than the grand prix category, that it chose to attack.

- The supercharged 8C 2.9-litre coupé of Raymond Sommer and Clemente Biondetti soon took the lead at Le Mans in 1938. It remained there safely until the Sunday morning, when it broke a valve, thus denying Alfa Romeo a fifth victory at La Sarthe. Alfa was never to win there again. *Motorsport Images*

- Alfa Romeo entered the 1953 Mille Miglia in force, with three new 6C Competizione Maggiorate. Consalvo Sanesi took an early lead only to crash. Karl Kling then moved to the front before also crashing. Juan Manuel Fangio, in the third (seen here), eventually took second place. *Motorsport Images*

Chapter 2
Birth of the Tipo 33

Rumours started circulating in early 1966 that Alfa Romeo was thinking of building an endurance prototype with a V8 engine. The company's CEO, Giuseppe Luraghi, wanted the marque back on the main stage of international motor racing, where it had strode so gloriously in the early 1930s and immediate post- World War II period.

The TZs, GTs and GTA touring cars that Alfa was then racing were all very well, but they had not brought back the glory days. Accordingly, Luraghi commissioned the company's Servizio Esperienze Speciali (SES) department to build a 2-litre sports racing car. It was to be known as the Tipo 33, for no other reason than this was a progressive design number for the long series of Giulia models. The prototype was completed in January 1965 and Luraghi wanted it to compete in that year's Targa Florio, but SES's Ing Livio Nicolis reckoned that a two-year development period would be needed before it could race. Autodelta's Carlo Chiti, who would be responsible for the engine, said that his company (see page 18) could make the car raceworthy on a much shorter timescale. Luraghi therefore decided that Autodelta would complete the car and so, not without controversy, the Tipo 33s became Chiti's babies.

The first car that he produced, a barchetta, certainly had potential. Designed by Alfa Romeo engineers Orazio Satta Puliga and Giuseppe Busso, it featured a light-alloy, Lucas fuel-injected, 1,995cc, 90-degree V8 engine. Its power output of 260bhp at 9,000rpm was certainly competitive at the time. The chassis featured an unusual design, with two large-section, light-alloy main sidemembers of cylindrical shape, linked by a similar main crossmember running across the car at the rear of the cockpit area. A large, snorkel air intake dominated the rear, leading to the nickname of the 'Periscopica'. Sad to say, the very dark red cars usually appeared at events in scruffy condition, and were unreliable. Jean Rolland, best known as a rally driver, was killed when testing one of them.

It could be said that the Tipo 33 won first time out, but this was at the supremely unimportant 1967 Côte de Fléron hillclimb in Belgium, with test driver Teodoro Zeccoli at the wheel. Other than that, at Sebring, the Targa Florio, the Nürburgring and Mugello, the cars failed to shine, looking ever scruffier as the season progressed, the only finish being a fifth place in Germany. The season ended as it had begun, with a victory but, again, an event of little importance, this time at Vallelunga, near Rome.

There was nothing fundamentally wrong with the Tipo 33's design, it was not as if they had been slow, so a new car, the Tipo T33/2, was designed for 1968, based on the original components. It featured a coupé body, stronger

- The story begins: the press launch of the prototype Tipo 33 at Balocco.
The Revs Institute for Automotive Research

- The inaugural outing for a Tipo 33 was at the Côte de Fléron hillclimb in Belgium. It was a strange preparation for the forthcoming Sebring 12 Hours. Still, it enabled Teodoro Zeccoli to win with the car, first time out.
The Revs Institute for Automotive Research

Carlo Chiti and Autodelta

- Carlo Chiti masterminded the Alfa Romeo Tipo 33 project. *Motorsport Images*

- 'The [ATS] cars were poorly prepared and seldom finished a race. It seems unlikely that the team will continue in 1964,' wrote author Mike Twite. *Motorsport Images*

Ferrari may have won the World Drivers' Championship in 1961 (with Phil Hill in the 156 'Sharknose'), but there were some unhappy people at Maranello. One was its chief designer, Pistoia-born Carlo Chiti. He left Ferrari, with five colleagues, to form what would ultimately become Automobili Turismo e Sport (ATS). Their intention was to build Formula 1 cars and sportscars, which would put Ferrari in its place. A new, and rather strange-looking, grand prix car was designed for the 1963 season to be driven by Phil Hill and Giancarlo Baghetti, who had won the first three Formula 1 races he had contested. So far, so good, but when the cars appeared, they were poorly prepared and the team was a shambles. To change the car's engine, chassis-reinforcing tubes running over the top of the engine had to be sawn, and afterwards welded back into place. The team competed in just five races before disappearing, the careers of its two drivers arguably blighted.

Carlo Chiti, though, soon bounced back and returned to one of his former masters, Alfa Romeo, for which he had worked on the Disco Volante and the 6C 3000 CM back in the early 1950s. He initially joined the Chizzola brothers in a new company, Autodelta, which was soon to become the competition arm of Alfa Romeo, initially working on TZ and TZ2 GT cars. It was an operation that he would rule in an autocratic manner.

Autodelta had its origins in a decision made by Alfa Romeo CEO Giuseppe Luraghi to create an external satellite operation for his company that would act as a racing department, and also assemble the Alfa Romeo TZ. Contact had already been made with Chiti prior to the ATS debacle, but he was already committed to that project. Luraghi then approached Lodovico and Gianni Chizzola, who had worked in the past in Alfa Romeo's own Servizio Esperienze Speciali (SES) department to build and race-prepare the TZs. Thus, in 1963, at Feletto Umberto just outside Udine, Autodelta was born.

Through Chiti, ATS became involved in the TZ's development, and when said company dissolved, he joined the Chizzolas at Autodelta. Luraghi then desired Autodelta to be moved to Settimo Milanese to be near to Alfa Romeo. Lodovico Chizzola did not want to make the move and so stepped away, leaving Alfa to take a share in the ownership of the company, with Chiti appointed as general manager. A major target was the European Touring Car Championship (ETCC), which under new regulations for 1965 would provide a title for the winning manufacturer, as well as the driver. A year later, Alfa Romeo would win the first of many ETCC titles. First up though, was to race the Giulia TZ2 under the Autodelta banner, which it did with some success.

This story, however, is about endurance prototypes, and Luraghi wanted to return to what he viewed as real racing. The result was the series of Tipo 33s, which, although the first was built by Alfa's own SES, quickly became the responsibility of Autodelta. From then on, and throughout much of the 1970s, Autodelta would become a major player on the endurance-racing stage. Along the way, there was the 1971 season in which the team won three World Championship races, two of them against the fearsome Porsche 917s, in addition to championship victory in 1977, but there were times when perhaps Autodelta's lack of preparedness reflected the earlier ATS operation.

There was also an involvement with Formula 1, Brabham using Chiti's Alfa Romeo engines to win two grands prix in 1978 with Niki Lauda. Chiti then developed Alfa Romeo's own cars for Formula 1, but the best results they achieved were three third places and a single pole position. It was hardly a reflection of the position Alfa had once held in grand prix racing.

A disillusioned Chiti left Alfa Romeo in 1984 to form Motori Moderni, building uncompetitive F1 engines for Minardi. 'He was very bitter', recalled Nanni Galli. 'If Alfa Romeo had been successful, it owed it to him alone.'

There is no doubt about the corpulent Chiti's engineering skill and astuteness, but his reputation had suffered with the debacle that had been the ATS Formula 1 operation. His organisational and administrative abilities were also questionable and these were things that Autodelta would be plagued with in the years to come. There are stories of success in these pages but, in the main, Alfa Romeo's return to sportscar racing was a failure relative to the glory days of the inter-war period.

Chiti died in 1994 following a heart attack. Nanni Galli is recorded, in *Alfa Romeo Tipo 33*, by Peter Collins and Ed McDonough, as saying, 'The problem was that he was an engineer, but as a man he had to do and be everything'.

Birth of the Tipo 33

The Tipo 33 of Andrea de Adamich and Nanni Galli, both of whom would race T33/TT/3 002, leaps around the Nürburgring in 1967. *Motorsport Images*

front suspension, increased front and rear track, and hip radiators located just above the rear wheels. In addition to the 2-litre engine, a 2.5-litre unit was also used in a few races. Privateers could now buy the car, and 28 were manufactured to enable it to be homologated as a Group 4 sportscar for the following season. A road-going model, the 33 Stradale, was also introduced.

Success at a meaningful level was achieved; starting with a 1–2–3 in the 2-litre class at the Daytona 24 Hours, following which the car was named after the banked Florida track. (A few weeks later a second driver, Leo Cella, was killed testing a T33/2.) Nanni Galli and Ignazio Giunti led the Targa Florio at one stage, before finishing second, and then went on to win the 2-litre category at the Nürburgring. A determined effort to win the Circuit of Mugello saw four cars entered, three of which retired, leaving the survivor, driven by Giunti, Nino Vaccarella and Lucien Bianchi, to win following a pit mix-up by the

Birth of the Tipo 33

● Six Alfa Romeos were entered for Le Mans in 1968, all of them 2-litre cars. Here, Mario Casoni leads Carlo Facetti on the Sunday morning. They would finish sixth and fifth respectively. *Motorsport Images*

leading Porsche. There was another win at Imola, where there was little in the way of opposition. Le Mans, having been postponed until September (due to civil unrest in France), was the last race of the season. Four T33/2s were entered, fitted with long, aerodynamic tails and tail fins. Considering how they had appeared earlier in the season, it perhaps came as a surprise that the cars were superbly prepared, with careful attention to detail. The result was another 1–2–3 in the 2-litre class.

While the T33/2 was now homologated in Group 4, Autodelta's focus for 1969 was on the 3-litre T33/3, which bore little resemblance to its predecessors. The H-section chassis had been replaced by a conventional monocoque, and the suspension was largely constructed from titanium. Large side-boxes contained foam-filled rubber fuel bladders. The new, light-alloy engine was a 2,998cc, 90-degree, fuel-injected V8. This had already been tested the previous year in a Cooper Formula 1 chassis, but it was to prove notoriously unreliable for some time to come. A six-speed gearbox was used for the early part of the season, but was replaced with a five-speed later. The Autodelta team was back to its scruffy, unreliable self and spent much of the year concentrating on development, which meant that the T33/3s were rarely seen in competition. There was a win in a non-championship race at the new Österreichring (Zeltweg) in July, but this was only achieved after Chiti protested that the Porsche that actually took the chequered flag first to 'win' had been pushed over the line by another Porsche after its engine had blown.

Chiti reckoned that by the end of 1969 most of the T33/3's teething problems had been resolved. The bodywork had been cleaned up, and a strong line-up of drivers had been engaged. However, 1970 was to be the year when the Group 5 monsters ruled the planet, the Porsche 917 having been developed, to be joined by the Ferrari 512. With hindsight, the Alfa Romeos did not stand a chance. On the tighter circuits, where the story might have been different, they were beaten by the 3-litre Porsche 908s. An improved version of the T33/3, with more extensive use of titanium for the engine components, plus revised steering geometry and lighter wheels, was first seen at the Nürburgring, and was used for the remainder of the season.

● There were no Autodelta cars at Le Mans in 1969. However, Count Van der Straeten's Team VDS entered a pair of T33/2s, both of which failed to finish. The 'Taf' Gosselin/ Claude Bourgoignie car, seen here, was fitted with a 2-litre engine, its stablemate with a 2.5-litre unit. *Alamy*

● The 3-litre Group 6 cars stood little chance against the larger Group 5s in 1970. Here, the Galli/Stommelen Alfa leads a Ferrari 512S round the tight Mulsanne Corner at Le Mans. *Motorsport Images*

Chapter 3
Enter the T33/TT/3

It seemed to take a long time but, come the 1971 season, Carlo Chiti had at last sorted out team management, while the cars were now quick and reliable. Perhaps not surprisingly, given this, the results began to come. The big Porsche 917s had overcome their Ferrari rivals and were still the cars to beat, but Autodelta did just that in the BOAC 1,000Kms race at Brands Hatch. With the 917s running into problems, Andrea de Adamich and Henri Pescarolo emerged as outright winners. More importantly for the Italian team, Vaccarella and Toine Hezemans won the Targa Florio – the first victory since 1935 for Alfa Romeo in the race that it had once dominated. In Sicily, the Alfa Romeos were every bit as fast at the Porsche 908s, all three of which were eliminated by accidents. To rub it in, de Adamich and Gijs van Lennep finished second in another of the T33/3s. It was surely the Tipo 33 series' finest victory, with the cars giving the Porsche 908s a hard time right from the beginning of practice. The fact that Nino Vaccarella, the man from Palermo and a hero to all Sicilians, was one of the drivers in the winning car made it all the more sweet.

'It is becoming more and more evident that, whereas Autodelta used to be a separate concern from Alfa Romeo, the Milan racing department is getting much more involved in the Tipo 33/3 project,' wrote *Motor Sport*'s Denis Jenkinson after the Sicilian race.

In addition to the three T33/3s at the Targa Florio, a fourth Autodelta car was present, 'with much drama,' said the press, although it did not race. This was the T33/TT/3, the TT standing for Telaio Tubulare or 'tubular chassis'. It was narrower, shorter, lower and lighter than the other T33/3s. The press described it as a virtual copy of the Porsche 908 – which Chiti admitted he had been impressed by – in layout and looks, with a central monocoque box-section and light-alloy tubular framework. In an era when designers had moved towards

- Henri Pescarolo rounding La Source at the wheel of the sole Autodelta car to start the 1971 Spa 1,000Kms. He and co-driver Andrea de Adamich finished third. *Alamy*

- The 1971 BOAC 1000 at Brands Hatch saw the first victory by a Tipo 33 at World Championship level. Here, winner Henri Pescarolo laps the Chevron B16 of Willie Tuckett. Many years later, Tuckett would become the co-owner of Alfa T33/TT/3 002. *The GP Library*

Enter the T33/TT/3

• The resounding Targa Florio victory of 1971 was achieved by Nino Vaccarella and Toine Hezemans, the former, a local man, regarded as the hero of the day. The Porsche entry was totally trounced and Alfa Romeo had won its first Targa since 1950. The next year would be very different.
Motorsport Images

monocoque construction, this may have seemed a retrograde step. However, the problem was that Autodelta simply did not enjoy the same level of technological expertise as Porsche, and its aluminium tubular frames proved to be dangerous. (Test driver Zeccoli had two accidents due to the rear suspension becoming detached.) Although the German manufacturer's 908/03s also had light-alloy frames, these were perfectly sealed and pressurised and a cockpit-mounted pressure gauge was fitted to give the driver fair warning of a possible crack or breakage. The Alfas did not have this system,

and thus a change was made ahead of the start of the 1972 season. The T33/TT/3s raced by Autodelta could be distinguished from the prototype, thanks to the input of Ing Gherardo Severi, by their safer, heavier, steel tubular space-frames. The aluminium-framed car was referred to as a Tipo 115.04, the steel-frame cars as Tipo 115.72s.

The new car had a short, 219cm wheelbase, with the driver sitting well forward. Interestingly, the gearbox was situated between the engine and the rear axle, instead of behind the latter. There were those who unkindly said that TT stood for 'Tipo Tedesco', or 'German type' because

Enter the T33/TT/3

Gijs van Lennep (seen here) and Andrea de Adamich finished runners up to the winning Alfa of their teammates in the 1971 Targa Florio, setting the seal on a famous victory. *Alamy*

When the first T33/TT/3 appeared in practice for the 1971 Targa Florio it featured an aluminium frame, unlike the steel-tube 1972 cars. Some felt it to be a copy of the Porsche 908/3. *The GP Library*

of its likeness to the 908. Writing in *Autosport*, Ian Phillips described it as 'a 908/03 painted red'.

On the Tipo 115.72's race debut the following year, *Motoring News* editor, Michael Cotton observed, 'The aluminium tubular space-framer of last year (it practised on five occasions but never raced) was used as a model for a steel-tube space-frame chassis which, Autodelta director Carlo Chiti explained, would be safer in an accident. It was certainly heavier, and the cars carried the additional penalty of the safety tanks, which had been in the news recently, adding 100 pounds in total (each 14-gallon tank weighs about 52 pounds more than a conventional one).'

When the prototype first appeared in Sicily, Chiti said that it was an experimental car, designed to take a new 12-cylinder engine, 'which may appear before the end of the season'. It was observed that there was room for such a unit.

There was no intention of racing the Tipo 115.04 in the Targa Florio, although it had been entered for Carlo Facetti and Zeccoli. It was simply there to gain experience of the car on the road. It was slower than the team's regular cars, and Rolf Stommelen described it as being too stiff. The car appeared again, with modified suspension, at the Österreichring, where it was driven by Galli and Henri Pescarolo. The former crashed it in the final practice session, taking off fellow Autodelta driver, Nino Vaccarella. Chiti was, perhaps not unsurprisingly, none too pleased. Pescarolo and Galli had both tried the car on new, low-profile tyres and had recommended that it should start the race, but that was prior to Galli's contretemps with Vaccarella.

The T33/TT/3 prototype appeared a third time, having been shipped across the Atlantic for the Watkins Glen Six Hours. Chiti, knowing that the rapid Vic Elford would be without a drive the following season following the withdrawal of the Martini Porsche equipe, was eager that he race for Autodelta. A carrot was offered by saying that he could drive the new T33/TT/3 at 'The Glen', which the Martini team was giving a miss. It never happened. During practice, a Porsche 911 got in its way and the car was, effectively, written off. Galli was again at the wheel.

A Tipo 115.04 also appeared at the Imola 500Kms, where it practised in the hands of Zeccoli. The Italian had been trying to get a tow from 'Clay' Regazzoni's Ferrari

Enter the T33/TT/3

Enter the T33/TT/3

- A drive through the countryside past crowded spectator banks for Toine Hezemans (seen here) and Nino Vaccarella took them to fifth place at the Nürburgring in 1971. *Motorsport Images*

- Watkins Glen saw a third victory for the Tipo 33/3, the winning car here in the hands of Ronnie Peterson. *Motorsport Images*

312PB when he arrived at a bend too fast, spun and hit the barrier, the car being too badly damaged for any more running that weekend. This sorry saga came to an end at another non-World Championship event, the Paris 1,000Kms at Montlhéry. Again, with no championship points at stake, it seemed like an ideal place for the T33/TT/3 to make its debut. Stommelen and Pescarolo were accordingly entered in the car. Suffering from too much rear brake bias and bottoming on the old circuit's many bumps, they qualified to start on the third row of the grid. It rained on the morning of the race, although the precipitation had stopped before the cars set off on the warm-up lap. Pescarolo, who later recalled that the team had no rain tyres available, tried a test start, spun the rear wheels and, encountering a change in the surface, charged the barrier and damaged the nose, rendering the car, again, a non-starter. It would not be until 1972 that the, by then modified, 'TT' would be raced.

There was to be one more win for the T33/3 that season. Porsche had emphatically gained revenge for its Targa Florio defeat on home ground at the Nürburgring, while Autodelta missed Le Mans, Chiti claiming that it needed a special car for such a high-speed event. However, at Watkins Glen, de Adamich and Ronnie Peterson scored a final win for the T33/3. With the season over, Elford and Stommelen then tested a T33/TT/3 at Paul Ricard under the guidance of Gherardo Severi. The engine was said to be producing a reliable 435hp and the engineer announced that he was very happy with the performance.

Given the fact that the up-to-5-litre Group 5 cars had still been legal, and the Porsche 908 had proved a particularly strong contender, it had been an excellent year for Autodelta. For 1972 there would be a 3-litre limit on all the world's major endurance sportscar races. The prospects for Alfa Romeo looked exceedingly bright.

The flat-12 engine that Chiti had promised was still not ready for the start of the season and so the decision was made to continue using the new T33/TT/3, but with the older V8 power unit. In addition to the steel tubular space-frame, several other changes were made from the prototype, with the front and rear subframes, various suspension components, engine connecting rods and steering column all constructed from titanium. Much was claimed for the foam-filled, fire-resistant fuel bladders that were fitted for the early part of the season, but they were quickly abandoned.

Alfa Romeo had high hopes for the season, but unfortunately, unlike Porsche, which had continued to improve the 917, Ferrari had stopped development of its mighty 512 in 1971 to concentrate on the forthcoming 3-litre limit, and would be taking on its fellow Italian marque with its compact, superbly engineered 312PBs that were to prove fast and reliable.

Part 2
The factory car

● The T33/TT/3's first appearance in a European race was at Brands Hatch, where Nanni Galli can be seen here driving the still-green-nosed 002. *Motorsport Images*

S heer, brute power had, for some years, been a feature of endurance racing. In the mid-1960s, Fords with engines of up to 7-litre capacity had arrived on the stage to wrest the sport away from Ferrari. An attempt by the Commission Sportive Internationale (CSI) to curb the monsters had failed. The prototype sportscars category, known as Group 6, was a division of the CSI's International Sporting Code, Appendix J, and the cars were to be restricted to 3-litre engines from 1968 onwards. Porsche and Ferrari then simply drove a proverbial coach and horses through that ruling. By manufacturing a run of 25 identical cars, they were able to legally pretend that these were not prototypes, but production sportscars (then Group 4, but later Group 5), which were allowed to have engines of up to 5 litres.

Despite the Group 5 era being now regarded as a 'golden age', the CSI was not amused. From 1972 onwards there would be no more games. The Group 5 racers were banned, and subsequently the front-running cars would be the little Group 6 prototypes, whose 3-litre engines reflected those then in use for Formula 1.

The changes appeared tailor made for Alfa Romeo, the team having scored three victories (as previously described), two of them against the leviathans, in 1971. A batch of new T33/TT/3s was prepared, based on the prototype that had appeared towards the end of the 1971 season, but with a significant modification to the chassis. One of those cars was 115.72.002.

Chapter 4
The Americas

● Following a torrid practice, Vic Elford found himself well back on the grid at Buenos Aires, alongside the little Abarth of Jorge Ternengo/Claudio Francisci, and just ahead of the old Porsche 908/03 of Juan Fernández/Jorge de Bagration.
The GP Library

In theory, the 1972 season held great promise for the Autodelta team. The big Group 5 cars had been consigned to history. The 3-litre Group 6 prototypes were now all that was needed to win, whether it be on Daytona's banking, around the confines of the Nürburgring, down the airfield straights of Sebring, or through the villages of Sicily. The Porsche 908s, which had once been the class of the Group 6 field, were now ageing and in private hands, and the drivers from the two semi-works Porsche teams were on the market. Two of them, formerly of Hans-Dieter Dechent's Martini International team, now found themselves paired to drive a new Alfa Romeo T33/TT/3, chassis 115.72.002, at Buenos Aires.

In signing up Vic Elford and Dr Helmut Marko, Alfa Romeo had added two of the best to its line-up. Elford had been one of the true heroes of the Group 5 age, while Marko had won the previous year's Le Mans 24 Hours, paired with Gijs van Lennep in a Martini Porsche 917.

'[At the end of 1971] we were all looking around,' recalls Elford. The question for Porsche's top drivers was whether they went to Alfa Romeo or Ferrari. Most seemed to be thinking the latter was the right direction; fellow Englishman, Brian Redman was certainly one who was heading to Maranello. During his time driving for Porsche, Elford had become close to the company's technical director, Ferdinand Piëch. 'We had a lot of trust in each other. I had a long talk with him one day and he said, "Do you know, Vic, maybe you will be better off going to Alfa because everybody is going to go to Ferrari and it will be an overcrowded bun-fight". That played largely in my decision to go to Autodelta. I thought I might be top of the heap, while I might just be an extra at Ferrari. In hindsight, he was wrong and so was I!'

Being part of the Autodelta team was, though, 'great fun,' says Elford. 'The only problem was that nobody spoke anything other than Italian. I could speak pretty good French by then and Chiti could speak French, as could one of the others. So, that was OK, except when they got excited! I learnt quite a lot of Italian during my year with Autodelta.' Vic was to describe Chiti as 'a kind of racing Godfather'.

9 January 1972, Buenos Aires 1,000Kms, Argentina
#2 Vic Elford/Helmut Marko, 4th

The first round of the new 3-litre World Championship took place at Buenos Aires in Argentina. The conditions in the Argentinean capital could be hot, very hot, and in the weeks preceding the race, temperatures had been over 100°F. Thankfully, by race day they were down to around 85°F, which was warm enough. All the major players made their way there, with the exception of JW Automotive, whose Gulf-sponsored Mirages, which were replacing the team's mighty Porsche 917s, were not ready. Rather stating the obvious, the press predicted Ferrari and Alfa Romeo to be the favourites. The latter, said *Autosport*, 'had a tremendous season in 1971 with [its] 3-litre cars and [its] experience should pay off handsomely this season'. Four cars were expected at Buenos Aires, 'fitted with revised V8 engines and the chassis has been lengthened a little'.

Speaking to author Maurizio Tabucchi, Carlo Facetti said that, with the deadline approaching for new cars to be built for the 1972 season, Carlo Chiti had asked him to try out the car at the Balocco test track. More than 20 days had been spent testing the first T33/TT/3 and now the Autodelta boss wanted his opinion. 'I wrote my report,' he told Tabucchi, 'highlighting the problems with the car and expressing my opinion that, as things stood, it wasn't competitive. This report of mine led to a meeting with Alfa Romeo, with the result that I was eliminated as a works driver.'

The Americas

Vic Elford was at the wheel of 002 when it made its debut at Buenos Aires in 1972. *whitefly.cc*

Unfortunately for Autodelta, the story of the 1972 season began as it was to continue. 'Alfa Romeo did not make a very convincing start,' observed *Autosport*'s Jeff Hutchinson. In the event, three of the new cars were entered, with the 002 chassis allocated to Elford and Marko – fittingly carrying race number two – the only one to finish. Even that was back in fourth place after a rather disappointing performance, which was made worse by a down-on-power engine that was only just running at the finish of the 1,000km race. It was even beaten by a 1971 T33/3 driven by Carlo Facetti and Andrea de Adamich, the Autodelta driver taking over the car from its Argentinean entrant, Giovanni Alberti, when his own T33/TT/3 retired with a damaged engine. (Facetti had called his friend Alberti to accept an offer of a drive once he had discovered he was out of favour with Autodelta.) Ahead of them all was a pair of Ferrari 312PBs; perhaps the season was not to be as promising as had been predicted.

Despite *Autosport*'s earlier comment, the number of 3-litre cars that turned up was disappointing thanks to the race being so early in the season calendar. Given that the T33/TT/3 had already been seen in prototype form, although never raced before, the only genuinely new cars at Buenos Aires were the yellow, Cosworth DFV-engined Lola T280s, which were said to be 'a very good match for Ferrari and Alfa Romeo'.

Compared with Ferrari, the Autodelta team was reckoned to be far from ready, so what was new there? Five Alfa Romeos were present: the trio of T33/TT/3s, plus a couple of T33/3s, one entered by the factory team, the other in the name of Alberti. In addition to Elford ('I loved Buenos Aires') and Marko, in what was said to be the lead car, the driver line-up for the T33/TT/3s was Rolf Stommelen/Toine Hezemans and de Adamich/Nanni Galli.

Following testing, Carlo Chiti had decided that the T33/TT/3s would feature a new 'long' chassis which, for safety reasons (as described previously) had been manufactured from steel tube. The new cars were, in reality, a mere 20cm longer that the prototype T33/TT/3. However, the steel chassis had taken the car just above the 650kg minimum weight limit. New fuel bladders had also increased the weight. When the cars first practised at Buenos Aires, the lightest of them weighed 709kg, but it was thought that it might have had more fuel on board than the Ferraris. The body shape and wheel sizes were the same as the original T33/TT/3 prototype, and the team ran the latest Firestone E1120-compound tyres at Buenos Aires, which had been developed for hot-weather conditions. Fuel and lubricants were supplied by Shell.

Development of the V8 engine had been given priority over the V12, and a tuning programme had taken place during the off-season. This had mainly concentrated on the cylinder heads and the engines were now said to be good for about 440bhp. Despite this, there was a lack of confidence in the engine's reliability, and seven spare engines were taken to Argentina for just five cars.

Preparation had been lacking, for although there had been a number of test sessions in Europe, none of the drivers had been given the opportunity to do any serious set-up work and, in Buenos Aires, were expressing disapproval at the way the new cars were going. Elford attempted to sort out 002 in Thursday's test session – when 50,000 people thronged the stadium – but was obviously disappointed with its handling following a number of spins. He did, however, manage to get the brakes working properly and, in addition, sorted out some softer springs ready for the first official practice the following day. Marko also spun several times that morning, following which he made suggestions to improve the handling. That was all very well, but then engine trouble intervened, which resulted in most of the Friday afternoon session being lost while the power

Vic Elford

Vic Elford's season with Autodelta does not reflect the Englishman's place in the pantheon of endurance-racing greats. It is too easy to run out of clichés for the men who drove sportscars during this era. Elford stands tall among them, every bit as quick in the fearsome Porsche 917s as Pedro Rodríguez or Jo Siffert. Elford would only take six major endurance victories between 1968 and 1971, but these tended to be on the tracks where outright speed had to be matched with raw courage. Thus, he won three times at Nürburgring and once at the Targa Florio.

There was, though, far more to Elford than just long-distance racing. Vic had reached the top in another motorsport discipline before he had even sat in an endurance car. It was in rallying that he first made his name, winning the then-prestigious 1967 European Rally Championship driving a factory Porsche 911. To prove he was equally at home on the circuits, he also won the 2-litre class of the British Saloon Car Championship the same year. Porsche saw that it was time to put its new rally star into a sports racing car that season and he made his endurance debut at the Targa Florio, finishing third in a 910 that he shared with Jochen Neerpasch.

The beginnings of 1968 were as glorious as they were varied. Within consecutive weeks, he won the Monte Carlo Rally and the Daytona 24 Hours race, the latter again with Neerpasch (also sharing the winning Porsche 907 with Hans Herrmann, Rolf Stommelen and Jo Siffert). Later in the year, he and Umberto Maglioli won the Targa Florio with a Porsche 907, while at the Nürburgring he partnered Jo Siffert to victory in a 908. He also made his debut in a World Championship Formula 1 race, finishing fourth in the rain at Rouen with a factory Cooper-BRM. No wonder fellow Porsche 917 driver, Gijs van Lennep reckons that Elford was the best all-round driver in the world at that time. (To add to the above, he drove in the first of three Daytona 500s the following year; it was very rare for a European driver to enter a NASCAR stock-car race.)

One of the true greats of endurance racing, Vic Elford spent just one complete season with Alfa Romeo. *Motorsport Images*

Listening to him, he comes over as one of perhaps only two drivers to have been unfazed by the dangerously undeveloped Porsche 917 in 1969. He and a reluctant Richard Attwood were six laps ahead at Le Mans, with only three laps to go, when their gearbox broke. A year later he was back with a now sorted 917, partnering Kurt Ahrens. He shot off into the lead, briefly lost it, but was back in front by the end of the first lap. That year it went wrong in the late evening, when a slow leak in a rear tyre caused handing problems. It finally ended the next morning with engine problems, but Elford had again shown himself to be a master of the long La Sarthe circuit. There would also be a second Nürburgring victory that year (still with Ahrens, but now in a more suitable Porsche 908).

When Hans-Dieter Dechent acquired the quasi-works

Much of Elford's time in sportscar racing was spent with Porsche, for whom he won the Targa Florio in 1968 with Umberto Maglioli in a 907. *Porsche-Werkfoto*

Porsches from Porsche Salzburg for his Martini-sponsored operation for 1971, Vic stayed with the team. That led to his final two endurance victories, both sharing with Gérard Larrousse, driving a 917 at Sebring and a 908 at the Nürburgring.

As recounted elsewhere, after consultation with Porsche's Ferdinand Piëch, Elford decided to go with Alfa Romeo for 1972. By his standards, it was hardly a satisfactory season, made all the worse by Jo Bonnier's accident at Le Mans. He would race on until a final appearance at Le Mans in 1983, but not at quite the same level. His final race win came in 1973 with an unexpected one-off entry in an Interserie race at Hockenheim, where he was given almost unlimited power in the Porsche 917/30 prototype. He was in his element.

The Americas

● The grandstands were packed at Buenos Aires, where 002, seen here again with Vic Elford driving, finished fourth.
The GP Library

unit was changed. It was during this period that all the fastest times were set, with Stommelen at least getting his Alfa Romeo flying to share the front row of the grid with one of the Ferraris. It became clear that the steel-tube chassis was a good deal stiffer than the alloy one and that the handling was suffering as a result. In an attempt to alleviate the problem, springs and anti-roll bars were progressively softened. However, it was only when he went back to harder springs that Stommelen was able to beat the two-minute-lap barrier.

But what of poor Vic and Helmut? They persevered throughout the Saturday practice session with another engine, but that was not much good either, and so they were well back on the grid, 13th fastest and even behind three of the 2-litre cars. It was obvious that they were not a happy pair.

At least 70,000 fans crowded into the stadium on race day. As if to prove what could be, Stommelen led the race away following a hectic session of tyre changing just before the start. Three Ferraris were on his tail, and these swept past as the German brought his T33/TT/3 into the pits after the second lap to have a sticking throttle seen too. He lost three laps as a result. Elford, in 002, had got up to sixth place, but he lost this when he too had to pit after just three laps. In typical Autodelta fashion, a screwdriver had been left rolling around in the bottom of his cockpit.

As the race neared the end of its first hour, the Alfa Romeos were poorly placed, the best being de Adamich's car in sixth place behind the three Ferraris and two Lolas. Stommelen, though, was showing what could be done, running with the leaders and keeping pace despite being several laps behind.

Matters became even worse when Galli was forced to pit shortly after taking over from de Adamich. He was quickly out again, but his car lasted only another 35 minutes before returning to the pits with water draining from its exhaust pipes. The Stommelen/Hezemans car then retired when a flat tyre sent the Dutchman, who had now taken over the wheel, into a guardrail. All that was now left of the T33/TT/3 challenge was a badly misfiring 002, although one of the older Alfas had now moved into fifth. There was now little hope for Autodelta for, back in sixth place, Elford was not going very quickly at all.

The situation did not improve when Marko took over, as he was suffering from severe flu and was completely exhausted. As the race progressed, so 002's performance appeared to deteriorate even further, but various retirements meant that there was a large gap back to the next car. Just by keeping going, it found itself in fourth place behind the older Alfa in which de Adamich had now joined Carlo Facetti. They were, though, four laps behind the leading pair of Ferraris, which were sweeping to an imperious victory.

In the end, the Alberti/Facetti/de Adamich car was slowed down to a safe finishing pace, completing the 1,000km six laps behind the two Ferraris, with Ronnie Peterson and Tim Schenken sharing the winning car. A further two laps behind the third-placed Alfa were Elford and Marko in 002. Autodelta surely had its proverbial tail between its legs. *Motoring News*'s Michael Cotton concluded that Ing Chiti, 'must be wondering now about the ethics of making his cars as safe as possible but slightly less competitive than rival makes; even two per cent on lap times makes a great difference in endurance racing'.

Vic Elford remembers, 'It was very frustrating to see how much quicker the Ferraris were once the season had started. Much as we all adored Carlo Chiti, he simply could not get it done.' However, with the next round at Daytona, and extensive testing at the Florida track prior to the race, Cotton could not imagine that Alfa Romeo would be so badly beaten again.

● The Ferraris were dominant at Daytona, as they were throughout 1972. Here, the three Alfas trail their Italian rivals and an Ecurie Bonnier Lola. *Motorsport Images*

9 January 1972 **Buenos Aires 1,000Kms, Argentina**
Round 1 World Championship for Makes

1	Ronnie Peterson (SE)/Tim Schenken (Aus)	Ferrari 312PB	168 laps
2	Gianclaudio ('Clay') Regazzoni (CH)/Brian Redman (GB)	Ferrari 312PB	168 laps
3	Carlo Facetti (I)/Giovanni Alberti (I)/Andrea de Adamich (I)	Alfa Romeo T33/3	162 laps
4	Vic Elford (GB)/Helmut Marko (A)	Alfa Romeo T33/TT/3 (002)	160 laps
5	John Hine (GB)/José Juncadella (E)	Chevron-Ford B19	158 laps
6	Juan Fernández (E)/Jorge de Bagration (E)	Porsche 908/03	157 laps
7	Gérard Larrousse (F)/Chris Craft (GB)/Reine Wissell (SE)	Lola-Ford T280	156 laps
8	Niki Bosch (E)/John Bridges (GB)	Chevron-Ford B19	156 laps
9	Nino Vaccarella (I)/Carlos Pairetti (AR)	Alfa Romeo T33/3	153 laps
10	Jacky Ickx (B)/Mario Andretti (USA)	Ferrari 312PB	152 laps

5&6 February 1972, The Daytona 24, USA
#5 Vic Elford/Helmut Marko, 3rd

Florida was blessed. There were 11 rounds of the World Championship for Makes in 1972 and two of them took place in the same US state. It had been thus since 1966, when the Daytona 24 Hours joined the Sebring 12 Hours contest, the latter having been the opening round of the then World Sports Car Championship since it was inaugurated in 1953.

The Daytona race had been emasculated for 1972, reduced for just this season to a six-hour event in accordance with revised FIA regulations designed to accommodate the new breed of sportscars with their Formula 1-sized engines. The weekend was still referred to as 'The Daytona 24' thanks to the fact that a couple of supporting races, for Formula Vee and GTs, were run during the 18 hours preceding the main event. *Autosport*'s Pete Lyons expressed the fact that this impressed nobody. 'Whatever atmosphere the race had enjoyed was gone. There were no 210mph coupés hurtling maniacally through the night. Instead, there

The Americas

The trio of Alfas at Daytona, with the Revson/Stommelen car leading, and 002 the meat in the sandwich. *The Revs Institute for Automotive Research*

were a few little three-litres – which used to be an also-ran category – rasping around the extremely artificial speed bowl about 25mph slower, and all in daylight. They are admirable little cars, but they are too well mannered to be exciting.'

Daytona was, and remains, something of a hybrid, making use of the track's high bankings, familiar to the NASCAR stock cars, along with an artificial infield for its annual sportscar race. Autodelta's drivers had been unhappy about the performance of the new T33/TT/3s in Buenos Aires but, after spending a couple of weeks testing at Daytona, lap times were thought to be showing promise, although one of the cars had been crashed. McLaren Formula 1 driver Peter Revson had been brought into the team, thus ensuring at least one 'local' if the New Yorker could be described as such. *Autosport*'s preview said that the pairings would be Helmut Marko/Vic Elford (in 002), Andrea de Adamich/Nanni Galli, and Toine Hezemans/Carlos Pairetti, while Revson would share with Rolf Stommelen. In the event, only three of these cars – chassis numbers 002, 003 and 004 – turned up from Argentina, two of them, as before, making use of Firestone tyres, the other, because of Revson's tyre contract, running on Goodyears. The fourth car was scratched from the entry following the testing accident, although *Motoring News* reported that Nino Vaccarella was to have been one of its drivers, not Argentine sports and touring car specialist Pairetti.

Things did not start well when the de Adamich/Galli car crashed in practice in what was to prove a harbinger of the tyre troubles that would plague Autodelta in the race. The chassis of the tubolare car was twisted, meaning that the pair had to switch to a 1971 T33/3 monocoque that thankfully had been brought along as a spare. With no Firestone 15in slick tyres available, the car would be handicapped by having to run on intermediates.

In an improvement from Buenos Aires, the green-nosed 002 proved to be second quickest of the Alfa bunch in qualifying, outperformed by the three Ferraris and one of the Lolas. That set the scene for the race itself. As the green flag was waved along the back straight, the Ferraris and the Lola flashed away, with the Autodelta trio in hopeless pursuit and the rest of the field nowhere, the second Lola (which qualified seventh, ahead of the T33/3 of de Adamich/Galli) having bogged down at the start. Not long after, a slipping clutch brought Tim Schenken's Ferrari into the pits, moving Revson up to fourth place, four seconds behind Reine Wisell's Lola. Behind Revson, Elford and de Adamich were circulating in close company, the 1972 and 1971 cars cruising at about the same speed.

However, it was not long before the front of the field went somewhat pear shaped. Leader Mario Andretti's Ferrari engine went sour and team-mate 'Clay' Regazzoni moved into the lead. The latter then slowed with a puncture, but remained out on the track as Wisell's Lola inexorably closed in. On the 27th lap, the British-built car was right up with the 312PB, but then the inevitable happened and the Ferrari blew a tyre. Its rear body flew adrift, and the Lola slammed into it. While Regazzoni spun luridly onto the infield, Wisell pitted to check the damage, leaving Andretti to regain the lead. Just after the one-hour mark, the American made a routine pit stop, during

● Helmut Marko and 002 on the flat at Daytona, leading Nanni Galli in the older T33/3. *George Boron*

the lead again as the Andretti/Ickx car was brought in for another unsuccessful attempt to rectify the misfire. Let us not, though, become too excited… It was not long before the Alfa also pitted and the engine cover was lifted to reveal a slipping alternator belt that took two minutes to replace.

And so it continued. The Schenken/Peterson Ferrari, now leading, also then suffered a puncture, while the old de Adamich/Galli Alfa Romeo had a front wheel bearing replaced. That was all good news for the subject of this book. Chassis 002 was running smoothly and was up to third place by the half way mark. The Revson/Stommelen car was, though, on its way to terminal engine failure and retirement. The last hour was trouble free for 002, Vic making a top-up stop just before the end, but still managing one fewer pit visit than the Ferraris, not that this made any difference to the final result. The car was four laps behind the winning Ferrari of Andretti/Ickx and two laps behind that of second-placed Schenken/Peterson.

which a spark plug was changed in an attempt to cure his engine's misfire. That left Revson in a perhaps unexpected lead, but he too had to stop and hand over to Stommelen, who proceeded to throw the Alfa around.

But what of Chassis 002 in all this? Elford was now in fourth place, behind the older Alfa, and was clearly trying to eek out his fuel to last around one and a half hours, which would mean just four routine stops instead of five. The Andretti/Ickx Ferrari and Revson/Stommelen, in the hardest-driven of the Alfas, were now disputing the lead, which was not how the race had been predicted. However, the Schenken/Ronnie Peterson Ferrari had by now come back through the field to challenge the second-placed Autodelta car. Then, in the third hour, the Alfa swept into

6 February 1972 **The Daytona 24, Florida, USA**
Round 2 World Championship for Makes

1	Jacky Ickx (B)/Mario Andretti (USA)	Ferrari 312PB	194 laps
2	Tim Schenken (AUS)/Ronnie Peterson (SE)	Ferrari 312PB	192 laps
3	Vic Elford (GB)/Helmut Marko (A)	Alfa Romeo T33/TT/3 (002)	190 laps
4	Gianclaudio ('Clay') Regazzoni (CH)/Brian Redman (GB)	Ferrari 312PB	179 laps
5	Nanni Galli (I)/Andrea de Adamich (I)	Alfa Romeo T33/3	175 laps
6	Tom Waugh (USA)/Hugh Kleinpeter (USA)	Lola-Ford T212	166 laps
7	Hurley Haywood (USA)/Peter Gregg (USA)	Porsche 911 S	166 laps
8	Robert Johnson (USA)/Dave Heinz (USA)	Chevrolet Corvette	163 laps
9	Roger McCaig (CDN)/Maurice McCaig (CDN)	Lola-Ford T212	161 laps
10	Jim Locke (USA)/Bob Bailey (USA)	Porsche 911 S	161 laps

The Americas

European interlude – Le Mans test day

The European season began for the endurance teams at the Le Mans test day in March. Weather conditions were more like June, but with the close proximity of the Sebring 12 Hours, the event seemed rather half-hearted. A four-hour race was also on the card for the weekend but, of the leading World Championship contenders, only one Lola T280 bothered to run. One of the new Alfa Romeo T33/TT/3s was present for the test, but Autodelta's performance seemed to mirror the whole season. As usual, the team was far from organised and, with Chiti at Monza for a four-hour saloon car race, the crew was telephoning him every time a decision had to be made. After the mix of tyres at Daytona, Autodelta had now signed with Goodyear for the rest of the season. This meant 13in wheels all round and smaller brakes.

The drivers present at Le Mans – Helmut Marko, Teodoro Zeccoli and Nino Vaccarella – reckoned that the handling had improved, while braking troubles now seemed to be in the past. The tail section of the car had been tidied up and made slightly longer. In addition, the rollover bar had been reduced to half the width of the car to save on unnecessary drag, and the radiators moved rearwards, just in front of the rear wheels, alongside the engine, instead of next to the driver, resulting in a neater body shape.

The centre of gravity was now much lower, which improved the handling. The car, though, was massively over geared and so no realistic testing could be carried out, with a top speed of just 182mph (293kph) on the Mulsanne Straight. Marko reported that he had been slipstreaming a Ferrari Daytona GT car to 'get by down the straight'. *Autosport*'s Jeff Hutchinson assumed 'the cars will undergo considerably more improvement at Sebring'.

● Autodelta turned up at the Sebring test weekend on 11–12 March with a pair of cars, one with bodywork unchanged since Daytona, the other with the radiators switched from the top to the sides of the body. All the Alfas raced at Sebring were so-modified, as can be seen here, this shot of Vic Elford showing the new, low, side NACA ducts.
The Revs Institute for Automotive Research

25 March 1972, Sebring 12 Hours, USA
#32 Vic Elford/Helmut Marko, Ret

Plus ça change, plus c'est la même chose. From Daytona's high bankings, the circus moved south through Florida to the airfield expanses of Sebring, but the change in terrain made no difference to the result. The highly organised Ferraris again finished in the first two places, with an Alfa Romeo a distant third.

The promoters, the Ulmann family, had promised a new track, but in reality it was still the same old bumpy runways used for the first-ever round of the World Sportscar Championship back in 1953. *Autosport*'s Pete Lyons felt he was back still further, in the 1940s. One could say that it is similar to that today. Whereas other former airfield circuits, such as Silverstone in England, have lost their airfield roots over the years as they have been developed, in contrast Sebring has never really shaken off its origins, thereby retaining a sense of history that others may have lost. Back in 1972, it was said that it

Helmut Marko

The 1970s saw a number of Austrians coming through the motorsport ranks. It was to be a story of triumph and tragedy, prefaced by Jochen Rindt's posthumous World Championship. Helmuth Koinigg was also killed, in what was only his third grand prix, while Niki Lauda's three world titles were blighted by his horrific crash at the Nürburgring. Helmut Marko, a school friend of Rindt's, had just 10 grands prix under his belt, all with BRM, when he was hit by a stone, thrown up by Emerson Fittipaldi's Lotus at the 1972 French Grand Prix. It pierced his visor, blinding him in the left eye and bringing about an end to his racing career. A few weeks previously had been what was surely his finest race when he hurtled around the Targa Florio circuit pursuing the leading Ferrari in Alfa Romeo T33/TT/3 002. Earlier in the 1972 season, Marko had recalled Rindt telling him that the longer they raced, the more chance they had of being in a 'dreadful accident'.

Helmut had joined Autodelta from Hans-Dieter Dechent's Martini International team. Although the 1972 Targa Florio may have been his finest drive, his greatest result came when he and Gijs van Lennep won the 1971 Le Mans 24 Hours, with Dechent's quasi-works, magnesium-chassised Porsche 917. Helmut was also successful in Karl von Wendt's 2-litre Lola T212 sportscar that year. Vic Elford has no idea as to why all his drives in 002 were with Marko, as they were never paired during their time with Martini Porsche. 'We had different personalities,' he recalls, 'so we were never cut out to be great friends, but driving together was fine.' By coincidence, when Marko lost his eye, Elford was driving the Porsche medical car that went to collect him.

Having cut his teeth in Formula Vee and then Formula 3, Marko also made his debut in both Formula 2 and Formula 1 in 1971, joining BRM for his home grand prix. He had previously failed to qualify Jo Bonnier's McLaren M7C for the German Grand Prix. He stayed with the BRM team until his Clermont-Ferrand accident, with a best placing of eighth at a wet Monte Carlo. He also finished fourth in the non-championship 1972 Brazilian Grand Prix.

Marko, who had obtained a doctorate of law from the University of Graz, his hometown, would remain in motorsport after his forced retirement from driving, working in driver management and also as a senior advisor to the Red Bull and Toro Rosso Formula 1 teams. He would also become head of the Red Bull driver development programme.

- Despite his hatred of the race, Helmut Marko's greatest drive was arguably at the 1972 Targa Florio. *Motorsport Images*

- The year before he moved to Alfa Romeo, Marko had, with Gijs van Lennep, driven a Martini International Porsche 917 to victory at Le Mans. *Porsche-Werkfoto*

might be the last race there because the track was so run down.

During two days of testing a fortnight before the 1972 race, cars had been practising and aeroplanes landing almost alongside each other. Vic Elford and Helmut Marko were again allocated chassis 002, and had trouble balancing the brakes that weekend. Marko liked more rear brake bias than did Elford. As a result, Vic had locked up and spun twice. 'Twelve hours is a long time and although the Ferraris are a little bit faster, we might have an edge of reliability,' Elford says on the soundtrack of *The Speed Merchants*, a film about the 1972 endurance season by Michael Keyser.

Autodelta entered four cars, with two older cars in reserve. Like the car at the Le Mans test day, three of T33/TT/3s had been considerably modified (the fourth remained in Daytona configuration) with the new body shells incorporating slightly longer tails and cleaner nose sections, and with water radiators mounted low down on each side of the engine, with side NACA inlets to feed them with air. As at Le Mans, the rollover bars did not give equal protection to both sides of the cockpit. This was a modification, which, later in the season, would be banned. One of the drivers reckoned the wheelbase had been increased, but this was denied. The handling did seem to have improved, but there were still a few problems, resulting in bitter complaints. The Alfa Romeos were again lighter than the Ferraris, and Elford (a winner here the previous year) and Marko, as at the test day two weeks earlier, were paired in 002. Lined up against the Alfas were the three Ferraris. For financial reasons, there was only one Lola this time, but the field had been joined by a new Mirage M6-Cosworth DFV from the Gulf-sponsored JW Automotive team, which had run but once before arriving at Sebring.

Qualifying saw Rolf Stommelen fastest of the Alfas, with a time in the first session that was good enough for third on the grid. Marko, though, shunted 002 into a hay bale on the Thursday morning, as did Nino Vaccarella with the unmodified T33/TT/3. There was much chassis straightening that evening, along with engine changes. Although the Friday qualifying sessions should have been an opportunity for faster times, nobody seemed interested. *Autosport*'s Pete Lyons said that Alfa persisted with its qualifying programme 'working hard in the hot sun'. Not all the Alfas were ready for the morning session – the Stommelen/Peter Revson car was now suffering engine maladies and there were still moans about the handling. Still, race founder Alec Ulmann was hosting a party the night before the race.

Come the start of the race, there were those among the spectators who still felt well enough after their own night's festivities to invade the track. That meant three pace laps before they could be dispersed and it was safe to get going, and as soon as the racing got underway the three Ferraris took off. Elford was initially fifth in 002 behind Stommelen's sister car. Alfa, it was observed, then had a gruelling race. Before too long, 002 was up to third place and cruising along quite nicely when its oil pressure dropped and the engine tightened up. Marko, who was driving it at the time, failed to make the pits before the engine seized altogether. And that, as far as the story of 002 at Sebring was concerned, was that. 'We thought we would win this one on reliability,' said Vic ruefully as the car was pushed away. 'It is a bad situation.' At the time, drivers did not always change their race overalls to suit the car they were driving, and Marko could be seen wandering down the pit lane in his Marlboro BRM Formula 1 livery, nothing left to do. Mario Andretti wondered what Helmut was thinking... 'Why, if the engine was going to blow up, did it take six hours to do it?'

The Andrea de Adamich/Nanni Galli Alfa had a rear tyre burst at high speed. The Revson/Stommelen entry, which had, during the first hour, been the first of the Alfas, stopped for a fuel pump to be repaired then, shortly after noon, Revson was black flagged following a report that he had overtaken under a yellow flag. The American denied this and lost his temper with the Chief Steward. Said dignitary's hat flew through the air and, although Revson then went on his way, he was subsequently excluded from racing any more that day and de Adamich took his place in the car. Eventual clutch failure rendered all the shenanigans pointless. In the end, the only Alfa left running was the Hezemans/Vaccarella entry, in third place, but a massive 26 laps behind the winning 312PB of Jacky Ickx and Mario Andretti. Towards the end, Hezemans was sure that his engine was going to blow up. As Elford said, 'The Alfas had disintegrated'.

● Chassis 002 could be easily distinguished during the early part of the season by its green nose. Here, Helmut Marko drives it at Sebring. *The GP Library*

25 March 1972 The Florida International 12-Hours of Endurance, Sebring, USA
Round 3 World Championship for Makes

1	Mario Andretti (USA)/Jacky Ickx (B)	Ferrari 312PB	259 laps
2	Ronnie Peterson (SE)/Tim Schenken (AUS)	Ferrari 312PB	257 laps
3	Nino Vaccarella (I)/Toine Hezemans (NL)	Alfa Romeo T33/TT/3	233 laps
4	Dave Heinz (USA)/Robert Johnson (USA)	Chevrolet Corvette	221 laps
5	Peter Gregg (USA)/Hurley Haywood (USA)	Porsche 911 S	215 laps
6	Gérard Larrousse (F)/Jo Bonnier (SE)/Reine Wisell (SE)	Lola-Cosworth T280	213 laps
7	Roman Pechmann (CDN)/Rudy Bartling (CDN)/Milt Minter (USA)	Porsche 910	213 laps
8	Luigi Chinetti Jr (USA)/Bob Grossman (USA)	Ferrari 365 GTB/4	210 laps
9	Daniel Muniz (MEX)/José Luis (MEX)/Ruben Novoa (MEX)	Porsche 914/6	207 laps
10	Vince Gimondo (USA)/Billy Dingman (USA)	Chevrolet Camaro	205 laps

Chapter 5
To Europe

16 April 1972, BOAC 1,000Kms, Brand Hatch, England
#7 Nanni Galli/Helmut Marko, 6th

Brands Hatch had been the scene of the Alfa Romeo Tipo 33's first-ever World Championship victory the previous year, but there was to be no repeat performance in 1972. Ferrari now clearly had the upper hand as the circus returned to Europe for the British Racing and Sports Car Club's BOAC 1,000Kms.

The UK's round of the World Championship was now a regular fixture at the Kent circuit, and while it perhaps lacked the charisma of Le Mans or the Targa Florio, it had seen some great racing, notably in 1970 when Pedro Rodríguez had performed what must have been one of the greatest sportscar drives of all time in his Gulf Porsche 917. However, it said something about the new sportscar regulations that only 15,000 spectators turned up on race day, compared to the previous year when 19,000 were present despite inclement conditions. Still, the undulating circuit, which had hosted its first World Championship Formula 1 race in 1964, had come a long way since its beginnings as a motorcycle grasstrack.

Autodelta arrived with three cars, the team already being described as the 'year's permanent bridesmaids'. The trio appeared as at Sebring, but with shorter rear bodywork. It was noted that the Alfas still had a greater frontal area than the Ferraris and Lola, which seemed to be a handicap on the fast circuits. The safety fuel bladders had been removed, at least for the time being, and improvements had been made to the suspension, leading to Helmut Marko claiming, 'I don't feel frightened any more'. Another 15bhp was said to have been found, bringing the total up to nearer the 440bhp claimed at Buenos Aires. *Motoring News* editor, Michael Cotton, mused that Autodelta was unlikely to be winning again until it had developed the flat-12 engine. Autodelta's Ing Gianni Marelli was reported to be doing more bench testing with the 12-cylinder unit that week, but was not committing himself in public as to when the new engine would race.

In a change to the driver pairings, Marko would share chassis 002 with Nanni Galli who, it was being written, was perhaps not as quick as his team-mates. Andrea de Adamich, wrote Andrew Marriott in *Motor Sport*, was fed up with being part of an all-Italian partnership, and so Vic Elford had been moved to share with him. Marko would be racing at Brands Hatch for the first time, and Galli had no recent experience of the longer Brands Grand Prix circuit. As far as *Autosport* magazine was concerned, the quick Alfas would be those driven by Peter Revson/Rolf Stommelen and by Elford/de Adamich. Opposition in the top class came from the three Ferraris with their stellar driver line-up, plus the Mirage M6-Cosworth DFV, competing in just its second race. Ecurie Bonnier had the only two Lola T280-Cosworth DFVs in existence, but this was said to be a shoe-string effort, the cars appearing travel weary and in need of some development testing. It was the first time that designer Eric Broadley had seen

● Helmut Marko at Le Mans in 1972, the last time 002 would race as part of the Autodelta team. *Getty Images*

● Work being carried out on an Alfa Romeo V8 engine at Brands Hatch. Another 15bhp was said to have been found now that the team was back in Europe. *Gerald Swan*

To Europe

● Little did Andrew Fletcher know that he would one day become the co-owner of the T33/TT/3 that he raced against with his Chevron B19 in the 1972 BOAC 1,000Kms. *Gerald Swan*

the T280s in competition. To add to these was a pair of old Porsche 908s, the more competitive of the two having been entered by Reinhold Joest.

Practice, observed *Autosport*'s pair of Richard Feast and Paul King, 'ran true to form'. The Alfa Romeos and the Mirage were reported to have been disappointing. In the wet Friday session, the trio of T33/TT/3s was behind the three Ferraris, with Revson the quickest of the Alfa drivers. All six Ferraris and Alfas, plus a lone 2-litre Abarth, were seen circulating together in a fast, red and seemingly patriotic convoy.

Saturday was dry, but cold, with the leading positions completely changing. New engines had been fitted overnight, but the Revson/Stommelen car was still the quickest of the Alfas. At the end of the afternoon, embarrassingly for the Autodelta team, the Lola T280s lined up behind the leading T33/TT/3, and the next up was a mercurial Arturo Merzario in the Abarth. It would not be the only time the little Italian would upset the team that season. Behind the Abarth came the Elford/de Adamich Alfa, while chassis 002 languished back in ninth, Marko having recorded a time of 1m 30.0s, Galli having gone round in 1m 30.8s. Michael Cotton wrote that a 'ragged looking' Galli had been blown off by the Abarth but, in mitigation he pointed out that 002's suspension had gone out of alignment when the engine had been changed overnight. Revson and Stommelen improved that afternoon to move up to fourth on the grid, but all the Alfas were slower than their predecessors in 1971. Come the race, chassis 002 would be way back on the grid, alongside the Mirage.

Once the Ford Granada pace car, driven by the new BRSCC chief Peter Browning, had peeled off, 22 chargers set off towards Paddock Hill Bend, with the Ferraris, not surprisingly, forging ahead. Galli started off in 002, still ninth as they plunged down the hill and then up again towards Druids Corner. Further up the field, Revson was having trouble with the Lolas which, when it came to speed, seemed to have the measure of the Alfas. Galli, observed Cotton, 'already seemed to be feeling the pace'. By lap 20, Nanni had moved up one place, but only because of the demise of the little Abarth, which had been giving the Alfas hell. At this point, 002 was the last car not to have been lapped, and the field was starting to dwindle in size. One of those retiring, with a wayward

● The 1972 BOAC 1,000Kms saw Helmut Marko racing at Brands Hatch for the first time. *Gerald Swann*

ignition lead, was the overheating Chevron B19 of Andrew Fletcher, who we will come across again later in the story of 002. The Lola challenge had come to an end by lap 96, and with both of the T280s wheeled away, Marko, who was now at the wheel of 002, moved up to a hardly meritorious sixth place. The race was starting to settle down, as Galli once more took the wheel. As Ickx and Andretti passed the 150-lap mark in the leading Ferrari, 002 was still sixth, five laps adrift. When Revson, in the first of the Alfas, came up to lap Galli, the Italian was slow to respond, so the reigning Can-Am champion gave him a nudge on the door, sending 002 skating across the grass and damaging the leading Alfa's headlight, not that the incident caused either party any major problems.

The Alfa Romeo stops, it was documented, were slower than those of the Ferraris. At 4.45pm, Marko shot into the pits for an unexpected halt and then waited eight minutes while the car's brake pads were renewed. It was the first unscheduled stop by any of the front-runners, and Marko's lap speeds slowed as he bedded in the pads, which meant that as he completed 187 laps, the leading 2-litre Chevron was just 36 seconds behind.

Meanwhile, the Ferraris seemed invincible as they swept past 200 tours.

There was, though, to be a twist in the tail, as Regazzoni's Ferrari engine went off-song. It took three pit stops before a replacement ignition coil cured the problem. By this time, the Ferrari had dropped back to seventh, behind 002, although it was soon to repass our Alfa, which in the last hour suffered from a loss of brake fluid. The pedal was going all the way to the floor, and Marko stopped again to have the problem investigated. More new pads were fitted, and an attempt was made to rebuild a front caliper. That did not seem to cure the problem, and with the next car on the road, the little Chevron B19/21-Cosworth of Francois Migault, catching up, the caliper was reassembled and Marko was sent on his way, which resulted in him having to stop every 10 laps for more brake fluid. This enabled the Chevron, which the Frenchman was co-driving with Brian Robinson, to overtake the Alfa.

It was only after the race that 002 was saved the embarrassment of finishing behind the 2-litre car. The Migault/Robinson Chevron was weighed and found to be 45lb underweight. The team pointed out that its car had been weighed before the race and found to be legal then, but the protest was to no avail. The Chevron was disqualified and 002 was promoted to sixth, having completed 220 laps, 15 fewer than the winning Ferrari 312PB of Ickx/Andretti and just two laps ahead of the 2-litre-class-winning Lola of Guy Edwards and David Hobbs. As Michael Cotton observed in *Motoring News*, the Alfa Romeos had been more competitive than previously that season, and they now appeared to be mechanically reliable, 'but they lacked the speed to make the slightest impression on the Ferraris'. It was hardly 002's finest hour; that was to come just over a month later.

What to do in the meantime? The cars were now reliable, but no match for the Ferraris on speed. Therefore, all Autodelta eyes were focussed on the Targa Florio which, pre-war, had been Alfa Romeo's domain. The team decided to miss the two rounds of the World Championship that came between Brands and the Targa, despite the fact that one of them would be on 'home ground'. Both Monza and Spa-Francorchamps were high-speed circuits but, as it turned out, the 1,000Kms race at the former circuit was held in the rain, so Alfa might, just, have stood a chance if it had turned up.

To Europe

Nanni Galli dives into Paddock Bend with 002 during the 1972 BOAC 1,000Kms. *The Revs Institute for Automotive Research*

16 April 1972 **BOAC 1,000Kms, Brands Hatch, England**
Round 4 World Championship for Makes

1	Jacky Ickx (B)/Mario Andretti (USA)	Ferrari 312PB	235 laps
2	Ronnie Peterson (SE)/Tim Schenken (AUS)	Ferrari 312PB	234 laps
3	Peter Revson (USA)/Rolf Stommelen (D)	Alfa Romeo T33/TT/3	233 laps
4	Vic Elford (GB)/Andrea de Adamich (I)	Alfa Romeo T33/TT/3	231 laps
5	Gianclaudio ('Clay') Regazzoni (I)/Brian Redman (GB)	Ferrari 312PB	220 laps
6	Nanni Galli (I)/Helmut Marko (A)	Alfa Romeo T33/TT/3 (002)	220 laps
7	Guy Edwards (GB)/David Hobbs (GB)	Lola-Cosworth T290	218 laps
8	John Bamford (GB)/Brendan McInerney (IRL)	Chevron-Cosworth B19	212 laps
9	Otto Stuppacher (A)/Kurt Rieder (A)	Porsche 908/02	201 laps
10	John Gray (GB)/Peter Gaydon (GB)	Chevron-Cosworth B19	199 laps

Andrea de Adamich

Although bespectacled Andrea de Adamich raced Tipo 33 Alfas on many occasions, he has only a bit part in the story of T33/TT/3 002, driving it just once. His Formula 1 career, in part, had similarities to that of 002's other Italian driver, Nanni Galli. He, too, experienced just one Formula 1 World Championship race in a factory Ferrari, retiring after a spin from the 1968 South African Grand Prix. He also finished ninth driving for the Scuderia in the previous year's non-championship Spanish Grand Prix (after a slow puncture). However, he was side-lined with neck injuries after crashing his Ferrari at Paddock Hill Bend in practice for the 1968 Race of Champions at Brands Hatch and, although he won the Argentine-based Temporada Formula 2 series for the team at the end of that season, he was not retained by the team after that.

Like Galli, he also drove the frustrating Alfa Romeo-engined F1 cars, and was a regular with the McLaren team in 1970, then March the following season. From then on he spent a couple of years with Surtees and subsequently Brabham. Although he started 30 grands prix, he finished in the points just twice, coming in fourth in both the 1972 Spanish Grand Prix and 1973 Belgian Grand Prix with, respectively, a Surtees TS9B and a Brabham BT37. He was more successful in non-championship events, with a second at Vallelunga and third at Brands Hatch during 1972. His Formula 1 career came to an end following the multiple accident that occurred after the first lap of the 1973 British Grand Prix, which left him with a broken leg.

Born in Trieste, Italy, de Adamich would drive in a host of disciplines, taking the 1965 Italian Formula 3 Championship, despite not winning a race. He was a regular with the Autodelta team, securing the 1,600cc class of the 1966 European Touring Car Championship for Alfa Romeo. He was at the wheel of the winning Alfa Romeo T33/3 for two of Autodelta's 1971 sportscar triumphs (Brands Hatch and Watkins Glen). He continued to race the Alfa endurance cars until the middle of the 1974 season when he quit the sport.

'He was not cut out to be a great driver,' says 1972 Autodelta team-mate Vic Elford, reflecting on how unusual it was for a Formula 1 driver to wear spectacles, 'but he was good.'

- A rare sight, a bespectacled Formula 1 driver – Andrea de Adamich. *Motorsport Images*

- Having been a Ferrari factory driver, Andrea de Adamich was back in grand prix racing with McLaren for 1970. Appropriately, this was to develop the Alfa Romeo V8 engine for Formula 1, but the season was a failure. *Motorsport Images*

To Europe

1 May 1972, Coppa d'Oro Shell, Imola, Italy
#40 Nanni Galli, 4th

The press was assured that the car Nanni Galli now raced in an Interserie round held at Imola in May was the one that he had driven at Brands Hatch. Thus, it looks likely that 002 made a one-off appearance in the Interserie championship, a European equivalent of the Can-Am series designed primarily for mighty Chevrolet V8-powered sports racers and powerful Porsche 917/10s. So, we now turn our attention briefly away from the World Championship for Makes and towards the Coppa d'Oro Shell.

The entry for the two, 30-lap-heat Imola races included a pair of Porsche 917/10s and eight McLaren M8s, as well as Galli's partner from Brands, Helmut Marko, now driving a factory-entered 8.1-litre BRM P167. Perhaps it was coincidence but, according to Jeff Hutchinson's *Autosport* report, it was the two Autodelta drivers who were the stars of the meeting – Marko through some determined driving of a troubled car, and Galli as the leading 'local' and in a 'David' of a car up against the 'Goliaths'.

It had been hoped that Galli would be driving a much talked about 4-litre, flat-12 Tipo 33. However, what arrived at the last minute was a conventional T33/TT/3 – his Brands Hatch car (002) it was said. Hutchinson mused that the late arrival was 'no doubt sparked off by Carlo Chiti reading the Saturday practice times in his daily paper and realising that he could stand a chance of winning this race better than he could against Ferrari'. Hutchinson concluded, 'He was right, too'. The car arrived just a few minutes before the final practice session, attended by Chiti and 14 blue-clad mechanics. Galli rushed out onto the circuit, returned to the pits a couple of times for tail-section changes and other minor adjustments, and then set second-fastest time.

At the start of the first heat, it was power that prevailed, Helmut Kelleners (McLaren) and Leo Kinnunen (Porsche) leading away from the Alfa. On lap eight, it all seemed to go wrong, as Galli went missing for a lap, but he was crawling round with a flat front-right tyre. This was soon changed and he returned to the same position in the field, albeit a lap down and now in 11th place. The Italian now proceeded to fight his way back to an eventual sixth place while, up front, the travails of others had left Willi Kauhsen (Porsche) in first place.

Early in the second heat, Galli became involved in a tussle for third place with Ernst Kraus (Porsche), George Loos (McLaren) and Marko. The Austrian blasted past them all and into the lead, while his Brands Autodelta team-mate moved up to fourth, but could make no impression on Kraus. There the Alfa stayed, while Marko remained in first place after a stirring drive. Having dropped out of the first heat with a suspected broken piston ring, Helmut failed to feature in the overall classification, in which Kauhsen was placed first and Galli fourth. The Alfa Romeo T33/TT/3s were not really suited to the Interserie, although one of them would appear at another round of the championship that October, when Andrea de Adamich borrowed a car from Autodelta to finish sixth overall in the two-heat Prix du Baden-Württemberg at Hockenheim.

21 May 1972, Targa Florio, Sicily
#5 Nanni Galli/Helmut Marko, 2nd

Alfa Romeo's relationship with the Targa Florio had been a glorious one. Following an initial win in 1923, the marque had totally dominated the dramatic Sicilian race throughout the early 1930s, winning on six consecutive occasions, Tazio Nuvolari, Achille Varzi and Antonio Brivio each taking a pair of victories. There was another win in 1950 and then a long succession of lean years. With the demise of the Mille Miglia, this was the race that Alfa Romeo really wanted to win again, an event on which Italian motor racing passions were given full reign. Carlo Chiti was anxious about this one.

In 1971, it all came right. With the big Group 5 cars uncompetitive around the Mediterranean island's twisting roads, Alfa Romeo followed up its win at Brands Hatch earlier in the year, Toine Hezemans and local man Nino Vaccarella leading home Andrea de Adamich and Gijs van Lennep for an Alfa 1–2. The determination was there to repeat this in 1972, despite the fact that Ferrari had won the first six rounds of the World Championship. There were grounds for optimism. Autodelta sent four T33/TT/3s, while Ferrari, after a certain amount of indecision, entered just one car, driven by its sportscar team reserve driver and a rally driver, albeit a first-class one, borrowed from Lancia. Alfa had even missed out on the championship rounds at Monza and Spa-Francorchamps to prepare for this race while, as far as *Motor Sport*'s Denis Jenkinson was concerned, the Ferrari entry was not much more than a gesture of goodwill by Enzo Ferrari towards the Sicilians and the Automobile Club of Palermo.

Chassis 115.72.002 was present for is sixth race outing. The drivers were the same as at Brands, Helmut Marko and Nanni Galli. Marko was a Targa Florio virgin, although he had been on the entry list to drive a Lotus Europa in 1968; Galli was an old Targa hand. The other Autodelta team pairings were Vaccarella/Stommelen, de Adamich/Hezemans and Elford/van Lennep, all accomplished Targa Florio racers. Vaccarella and Elford particularly enjoyed the event, Nino beloved of the Sicilians and Vic because it was so similar to the discipline of rallying in which he had cut his teeth. Marko, by contrast, made clear his objections to what was, after all, a particularly dangerous race. He did not like it; he did not want to do it, and stated that he would not be coming back the following year.

Only minor changes had been made to the cars since their last outings. The radiator air intakes were now only on the tops of the doors. The air outlets were at the side instead of the top of the bodywork, both improving the cooling and reducing the chances of ingesting the muck that tended to line the Targa circuit. There was also a camshaft alteration, improving power from 5,000rpm. As far as handling was concerned, the rear suspension had been slightly altered, with a different top-link mounting. This lowered the roll centre and provided more camber change, giving more traction on the slippery Sicilian road surfaces. 'The suspension,' wrote Michael Cotton in *Motoring News*, 'had been softened to an almost ridiculous degree.' Vaccarella got the body of his car to scrape along the road when cornering, at which point Chiti realised that the limit had been reached and put stiffer springs on.

Other than the Alfas, the only other car in the 3-litre prototype category was the Arturo Merzario/Sandro Munari Ferrari 312PB. Otherwise, there was a diverse 2-litre Group 5 class, various other smaller sportscars, and a Porsche-dominated GT group in the 76-strong entry.

The week did not begin well for anyone, with the Palermo and Trapani firemen on strike for higher pensions. As the local fire services were refusing to man

The Targa pits, with 002 bearing race No 5. Ahead of the Galli/Marko car is the No 4 T33/TT/3 of de Adamich/Hezemans, with the No 1 car of Vaccarella/Stommelen in the background.
Getty Images

the circuit with full equipment, the Thursday official practice session was cancelled, and firemen from other parts of the island were brought in for a four-hour Saturday-morning practice session. However, this lost much of its significance when it was decided that the starting order should be drawn by lot, rather than decided by practice times. Most of the professional drivers had in any case been thrashing around the circuit in Hertz and Avis hire cars during the preceding days. The busy streets of Cerda, Campofelice and Collesano had even echoed to the sound of a 3-litre prototype from time to time. Practice for the Targa Florio had its own meaning.

Conditions that Saturday morning were slippery, little resurfacing having been done since the previous year. Marko was the first to take out 002, recording a time of 35m 44.0s. This proved to be the slowest time set by an Alfa. Quicker than all of them, which was no surprise given how the season had gone so far, was the Ferrari.

Speaking to *The Red Bulletin* magazine many years later, Marko said that the first few laps were a shock: 'During practice Toine Hezemans collided with a donkey, rider and all. He was catapulted over the rear spoiler. Nino Vaccarella and his car disappeared under a truck. One car got lost in the mountains. It took half a day just to find it again. There were no crash barriers, just outsized bales of hay here and there.'

Race day was cloudless, the high winds that had plagued the island earlier in the week having disappeared, and the sun had become uncomfortably hot by the beginning of the race. Galli was the start driver for now yellow-nosed 002, leaving the line fourth, one minute after Merzario in the Ferrari. One lap later, and it was looking bleak for Autodelta. Elford, who had been first away – a dubious privilege as it made him a hare for the hounds – was out due to a hole in the side of his car's V8 engine block, while Merzario had already made up more than a minute on de Adamich (who had started second) and was leading both on the road and on elapsed time. 'Chiti had built me a special engine, knowing my record on the Targa,' recalls Elford, 'and I was really flying. I went up through Cerda and, as I came down through the long main straight into Campofelice, I knew I was way ahead. I obviously did not know by how much, but I knew the timing that I was doing in my mind. It was a lovely, bright

Nanni Galli was forced into a spin in his battle with Sandro Munari during the 1972 Targa Florio. *www.motoprint.co.za*

sunny day, the car was beautiful and the engine seemed to be a dream. Suddenly, out of this bright blue sky, it was raining. I thought, "That's odd," but then I realised that the "rain" was hot. The engine had blown a hole in itself and I was being showered with my own cooling water.' Elford parked the car which, in a few minutes, was covered in local children.

Galli, in 002, was third on the road, but actually in second place, having lapped faster than his remaining Alfa team-mates. Merzario sped off into the distance over the second lap, while Galli dropped back behind the other Alfa after pitting for fuel and front tyres and handing over to Marko. Now things began to look better for Alfa. Marko began to lap faster than anyone, while Ferrari botched a pit stop, its skeleton crew made up mainly of new recruits. Chassis 002 took the lead on time on lap four, which Marko completed in 34m 15.1s. On the road, the Austrian was in third place, hot on the heels of team-mate Hezemans, who was about five seconds adrift of the Ferrari, now driven by Munari. Although the cars had started at 15-second intervals, there was now a real fight on the road, and the spectators were cheering wildly around the 72km circuit.

Hezemans then hit a rock and broke a wheel, which effectively put his Alfa out of contention, so the contest was now a straightforward matter of 002 versus the Ferrari. With the half-distance mark reached, Marko started to rise to the challenge, breaking the 34-minute lap barrier for the first time.

Ferrari discipline does not seem to have been too good that day. Munari, who was ahead on the road, albeit now second on time, saw a sign at the Polizzi signalling

- An everyday scene in a Sicilian town centre, with Helmut Marko driving past the locals. *The GP Library*

post intended for Marko, mistook it for one intended for him, and pitted a lap early. Both the Ferrari and Marko's Alfa dived in the pits at the same time, giving the crowd more cause for excitement. Marko handed over to Galli while new rear tyres were fitted in a stop which took 52 seconds, and 002 left the pits five seconds ahead of the Ferrari, which meant that it was now a minute in the lead on corrected time. No one in the Ferrari pit had been expecting Munari, and Merzario had to grab his crash helmet before taking over their car.

The little Italian was now driving the 312PB like a man inspired. Galli thought that once he had been caught on the road by the Ferrari he would be able to stay with it, thus maintaining his one-minute lead. There was no such chance. Arturo was off into the distance, carving a gap of 100 seconds over the Alfa in just one lap. The Ferrari team decided to split the rest of the race into two-lap stints, calculating that the way Merzario was going, there would be enough time to change tyres, refuel and swap drivers.

However, the Ferrari team should have realised it was not having one of its better days as far as pitting was concerned. The pit direction of former team manager Peter Schetty (who had now retired to deal with family business) was being sorely missed. Merzario hit Gianfranco Bonetto – who was waiting to take over the then-third-placed Chevron – as he pitted, injuring Bonetto's knee. By the time the Ferrari left, now in the hands of Munari, it was just a few seconds ahead of Galli on the road and almost a minute behind on elapsed time. On full fuel tanks, Munari was likely to lose more time. At that point, God proved to be on the side of Maranello.

- Galli's Alfa show signs of rear-end damage as he presses on past the crowds in Sicily. www.motoprint.co.za

Alfa Romeo T33/TT/3

To Europe

Helmut Marko charges on through the Sicilian countryside. *Alamy*

Munari came across a Lancia Fulvia, which he slipped past. Galli was coming up fast, but before he too could lap the Lancia, it spun in front of him. Galli was forced to spin his own car to avoid crashing into it. His engine promptly died, and he spent two minutes restarting it. The result was that, when he pitted at the end of lap eight, he was two and three quarter minutes behind on the road. Marko, who was beside himself with anxiety, now took over, but by the time he left the pits, more time had been lost and he was now three and a half minutes in arrears. It was observed that Helmut had lifted his co-driver from the car almost as the wheels had stopped turning.

Those final three laps saw what was perhaps one of Helmut Marko's best drives, a poignant thought given that his racing career was shortly to come to an end following an accident at the French Grand Prix. All through lap nine, Marko was catching rallyman Munari, who would soon have to stop to hand over to Merzario for the final two laps. This time, the Ferrari pit was on the ball, and took just 30 seconds, leaving 'Art' 2m 50s ahead on the road, but a minute less than that on corrected time. Marko continued to throw 002 around and, with a lap of 33m 54.8s, took 70 seconds out of the Ferrari lead. With just one of the Targa's lengthy laps to go, he was only 38 seconds behind. The four Ferrari signalling points around the circuit responded and exhorted Merzario to go faster, but he was suffering from an upset stomach caused by too much ice-cold drink consumed during his rest period. Helmut was as one possessed. At Caltavutaro, 002 was just 32 seconds behind the Ferrari, at Polizzi the gap was down to 28 seconds, by Collesano it was 20 seconds and by Campofelice it was 12 seconds. The 1972 Targa Florio may have been lacking in numbers when it came to the front runners, but two of them were making it one of the most exciting races in the event's 66-year history.

The Ferrari had a slight edge on top speed, something that Marko could not really combat, despite his spectacular handling of the Alfa. On the straight before Cerda, Merzario made use of this and, by the time he had reached the finish line, had eeked out his lead slightly to 17 seconds. He hit the brakes as he crossed the line and almost collapsed. Would Marko arrive within the next minute? All eyes looked down the road, but the 60 seconds passed; Merzario and Munari had scored a famous victory. Seventeen seconds later, a frustrated and dejected Marko stormed in to great cheers. It had been so near and yet so far for chassis 002 and its best opportunity to go down in motorsport history.

Perhaps that last statement is a little unfair, 002 did claim its place in the annals of motor racing. Marko's final lap of 33m 41.0s – a speed of 79.69mph (128.25kph) – was the quickest of the day, just five seconds short of the blindingly fast record set by Leo Kinnunen in a Porsche 908 two years earlier. *Autosport* even had it erroneously down as the lap record in its results, although rival 'weekly' *Motoring News* recognised the Finn's earlier achievement. The following year, it would be another Alfa Romeo that set fastest lap, but the T33/TT/12 of Rolf Stommelen did not manage to break the 34-second mark. Perhaps there was something numerically appropriate in Marko's T33/TT/3 blasting round in just over 33 minutes.

In the event, Marko had given his all, driving as he said that evening like a man possessed. 'Your whole body was battered and bruised after a sportscar race,' he reflected many years later. 'Driving these cars was extremely hard physically.'

21 May 1972 **Targa Florio, Sicily**
Round 7 World Championship for Makes

1	Arturo Merzario (I)/Sandro Munari (I)	Ferrari 312PB	11 laps
2	Nanni Galli (I)/Helmut Marko (A)	Alfa Romeo T33/TT/3 (002)	11 laps
3	Andrea de Adamich (I)/Toine Hezemans (NL)	Alfa Romeo T33/TT/3	11 laps
4	Antonia Zadra (I)/Enrico Pasolini (I)	Lola T290-Cosworth	10 laps
5	Gabriele Gottifredi (I)/Pino Pica (I)	Porsche 911 S	10 laps
6	Günter Steckkönig (D)/Giulio Pucci (I)	Porsche 911	9 laps*
7	Giuseppe Virgilio (I)/Luigi Taramazzo (I)	Abarth 2000	9 laps*
8	Maurizio Zanetti (I)/Ugo Locatelli (I)	Lola-Alfa T212	9 laps
9	Dieter Schmid (D)/Armando Floridia (I)	Porsche 914/6	9 laps
10	Jürgen Barth (D)/Michael Keyser (USA)	Porsche 911 S	9 laps

*DNF

Nanni Galli

Nanni, or more correctly Giovanni (he had hoped to hide his racing from his family with a pseudonym), Galli came from a wealthy Bolognese family. In the mid 1960s, he showed promise as a serial winner of national races in a Mini Cooper S. He joined Alfa Romeo in 1967 to race both touring and sportscars, and was seen at the wheel of a Tipo 33 every season from then until 1972, when he raced T33/TT/3 chassis 002 in a couple of World Championship rounds, plus possibly the Interserie race at Imola. Despite this lengthy period with these cars, his only win of note was in the 1968 non-championship Gran Premio de Mugello (run for sportscars), when he shared a T33/2 with Lucien Bianchi and Nino Vaccarella. He left Alfa in 1972 after, he recalled, 'arguing with Ing Bardini over a crash with the 33'. It was, though, he said, 'incredible to race with Autodelta' and he felt that Chiti had been like a father to him.

In 1968, he moved into single-seater racing with a Formula 2 Brabham-Alfa Romeo BT23 and then, the following season into Formula 1, failing to qualify a factory McLaren M7D – also with an Alfa engine – for the Italian Grand Prix. The 1971 season saw him with March, sometimes using Alfa Romeo power, sometimes a Cosworth DFV, the idea having been to develop the Italian V8. There were two more seasons in Formula 1, the first of these with Tecno, for whom he had raced in Formula 2 back in 1969. Although the Bologna-based manufacturer had been successful in the lower formulae, it struggled at the top level with its flat-12-engined, Martini-backed car. Galli did, though, finish third in a poorly supported, non-championship race at Vallelunga. Nanni also had a one-off drive for Ferrari in 1972 – surely every Italian racer's dream – in the French Grand Prix, standing in for the injured 'Clay' Regazzoni. The Ferrari team was in disarray at the time and he finished in 13th position. He moved on to Williams for 1973, driving the team's ISO Marlboro-Cosworth DFV, but retired from driving before half the season was over, disillusioned with yet another uncompetitive car.

Fellow 002 pilot Vic Elford recalled that, of all the Alfa Romeo drivers in 1972, Galli was the only one that he really knew. 'He was a very good driver. He did not make many mistakes.'

Galli was to follow his father into the clothing business, establishing the Fruit of the Loom brand. He would also later return to racing, competing in historic-car events and bringing with him, as Tim Samways puts it, 'a lot of knowledge of racing these cars in period'. Samways' racecar-preparation business ran him in Gianluca Rattazzi's Alfa Romeo T33/3 before sickness curtailed Nanni's participation. He died in October 2019 after a long illness.

- Nanni Galli was a long-term Alfa Romeo driver, first racing for the marque in 1967, in both saloon and endurance cars. *Motorsport Images*

- Like de Adamich, Galli was called upon to help develop the Alfa Romeo V8 for Formula 1. In 1971, he was placed with the March team, which had taken over the project, but could do no better that 15th place in the Austrian Grand Prix. He is seen here at Monza, where he retired with electrical maladies. *Motorsport Images*

To Europe

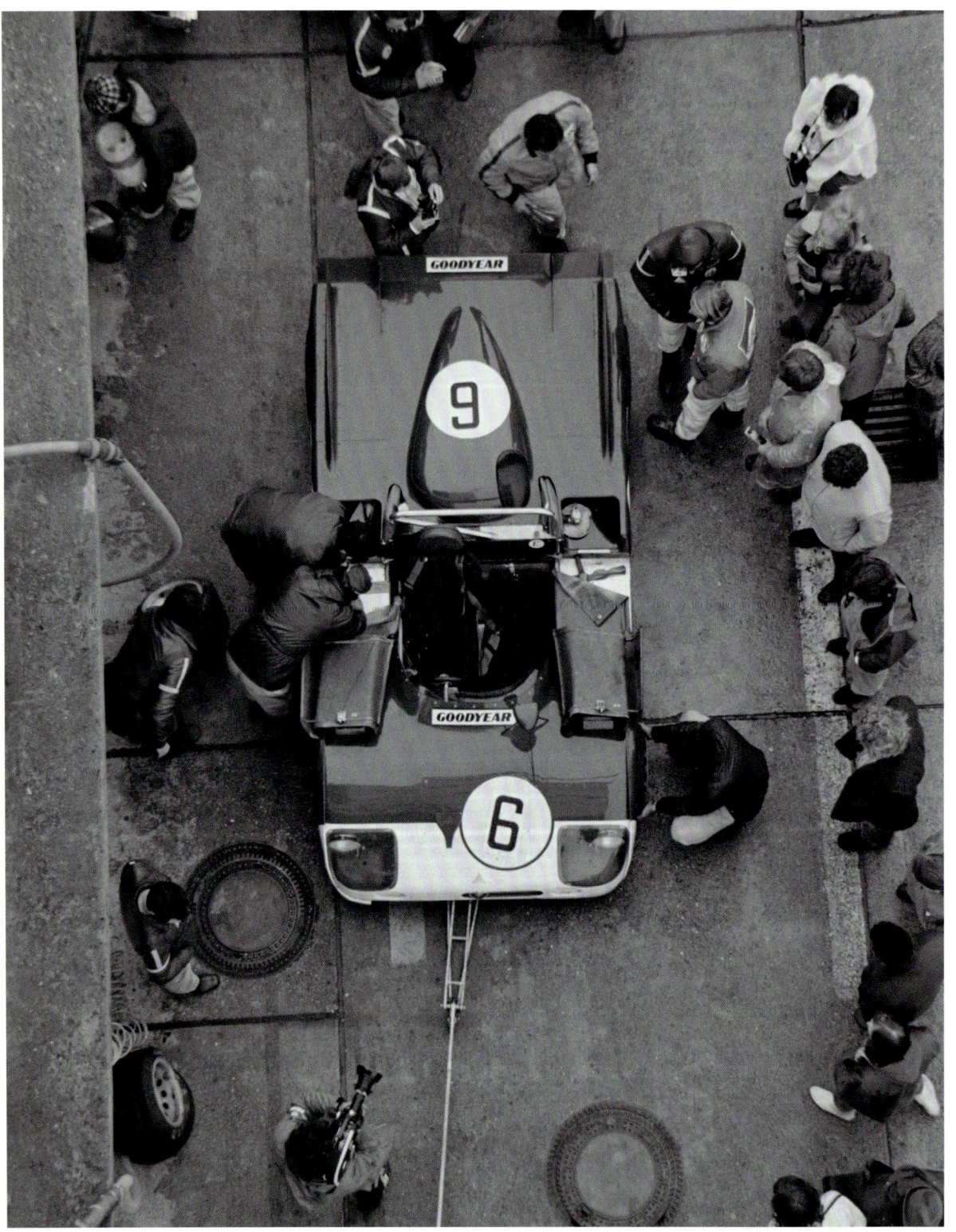

The Alfa pit seen from above at the Nürburgring, where 002 was driven by Marko and de Adamich.
The Revs Institute for Automotive Research

28 May 1972, ADAC-1,000Kms-Rennen, Nürburgring, Germany
#6 Helmut Marko/Andrea de Adamich, 3rd

As *Autosport*'s editorial pointed out at the time, the Targa Florio had been the one race in which the Alfa Romeo team had hoped to save some face and avoid a total whitewash, and it had failed. However, the magazine had some sympathy for Autodelta. 'Despite [its] defeats [it] has entered most rounds enthusiastically and hopefully, but it is evident that [its] V8s are not competitive enough.'

Four more rounds of the World Championship remained, starting with the Nürburgring 1,000Kms, still in those days on the demanding, 14-mile long Nordschleife. Alfa was expected to send at least three cars. A trio of T33/TT/3s turned up, including 002 – which had, once again, changed the colour of its nose, it was now white – but only two of them made the race. It was said that Nanni Galli had let the side down on the Targa Florio and had been asked not to go to Germany. Vic Elford, who was flying back and forth to England, as he was scheduled to drive in a Formula 2 race at Crystal Palace on the Monday, was now teamed up with Rolf Stommelen in what was described as 'the stronger pair'. Chiti said that Vic could drive the middle part of the race in order to catch an aeroplane. Helmut Marko still had 002, but was now joined by Andrea de Adamich in what would be the Italian's only race in this particular chassis. Little had

● A variety of 3-litre prototypes at the start of the Nürburgring 1,000Kms. Front row (left to right): Ferrari (Peterson/Schenken) and Mirage (Bell/van Lennep). Second row: Alfa Romeo (Stommelen/Elford), (Marko/de Adamich). Third row: Porsche (Joest/Casoni) and Ferrari (Merzario/Redman). Also in the picture is a third Ferrari (Ickx/Regazzoni) and a pair of 2-litre Chevrons.
The Revs Institute for Automotive Research

been changed on the two cars, apart from the fitment of large rear fins and a few aerodynamic tweaks.

The Nürburgring race was notable for the fact that there was a challenge to the Ferrari supremacy, but it came from the now well-developed Mirage that even led for a short period before dropping out. One of the Ferraris crashed, which enabled one of the Alfas to reach the podium again, chassis 002 being, once more, Autodelta's most successful car, in third place.

The overall entry for the race was huge, but the 3-litre prototypes were just eight in number. Coincidentally, eight hours were allocated for practice, but it rained for much of that time. For only a few minutes on the Saturday morning was any of the circuit dry. Few people bothered with the Friday session, but during a period when the track was less flooded, Marko did go out to record second-fastest time of the day. He was late out on the Saturday, and then spent much of the time driving the spare car, the engine of which was misfiring. This did not matter, as he would be transferring to 002 for the race. The conditions meant that the two-by-two grid had an unusual look about it, with just one of the Ferraris on the front row, alongside the Mirage, and with the Alfas next up, 002 being the slower of the two.

About half an hour before the race, it started to rain. The roads through the Eifel mountains were treacherous enough without also being slippery.

To Europe

Marko is seen here driving 002 at the Nürburgring, where conditions were far from ideal. *The Revs Institute for Automotive Research*

A rolling start saw Marko initially in sixth place. As the track dried, so the Ferraris and the Mirage pulled away from the Alfas, while 002 seemed to be losing contact with the other T33/TT/3. Marko was not finding life easy thanks to an inoperative rev counter and a sticking throttle.

Autodelta was performing true to form, and the Alfa Romeos' first pit stops were long and unpolished. Indeed, a 2-litre Lola managed to get ahead of 002 when de Adamich was on his first lap out of the pits. The Marko/de Adamich car did, though, then move up the field, but not due to its own efforts. Elford, in the first of the Alfas, had stopped when his front-left wheel fell off. It seemed that it had not been tightened properly during a tyre change. Although Vic was eventually able to continue he, understandably, seemed to have lost interest.

On lap 18, de Adamich stopped to hand 002 back to Marko and for a tyre change. The car was, though, almost a lap behind the leaders, and a lap at the Nürburgring was a very long way.

The story of the second half of the race was of further challenge to the two remaining Ferraris ('Clay' Regazzoni had crashed his 312PB) from Derek Bell and Gijs van Lennep in the Mirage, until gear-selection trouble got to the Gulf car. Bell was also feeling unwell and was sick in his helmet. With the 312PB of Ronnie Peterson and Tim Schenken leading, Arturo Merzario, in the second Ferrari, was catching the Mirage fast, but it seemed as if the Englishman might still hang on to second place until, with two laps left, the Mirage's Cosworth engine blew. However, the field was sufficiently strung out that only one car was able to make up the deficit to the stationary Mirage. That was 002, which thus inherited third place, a lap down on the winning Ferrari. Elford listened to the end of the race on a car radio on his way to the airport.

28 May 1972 ADAC-1,000Kms-Rennen, Nürburgring, Germany
Round 8 World Championship for Makes

1	Ronnie Peterson (SE)/Tim Schenken (AUS)	Ferrari 312PB	44 laps
2	Arturo Merzario (I)/Brian Redman (GB)	Ferrari 312PB	44 laps
3	Helmut Marko (A)/Andrea de Adamich (I)	Alfa Romeo T33/TT/3 (002)	43 laps
4	Derek Bell (GB)/Gijs van Lennep (NL)	Mirage M6-Cosworth	42 laps
5	John Hine (GB)/John Bridges (GB)	Chevron B19/21-Cosworth	41 laps
6	Gérard Larrousse (F)/Jo Bonnier	Lola T290-Cosworth	39 laps
7	Dieter Glemser (D)/Jochen Mass (D)	Ford Capri RS 2600	38 laps
8	Hans-Joachim Stuck (D)/Alex Soler-Roig (E)	Ford Capri RS 2600	38 laps
9	John Fitzpatrick (GB)/Erwin Kremer (D)	Porsche 911 S	38 laps
10	Günter Steckkönig (D)/Dieter Schmid (D)	Porsche 911 S	37 laps

11 June 1972, Le Mans 24 Hours, Le Mans, France
#17 Vic Elford/Helmut Marko, Rtd
During the early 1930s, Alfa Romeo became one of the great marques of the Le Mans story. The hitherto all-conquering 'works' Bentleys had withdrawn from competition after 1930 and there was a marked contrast to previous years in the entry for the 1931 24 Hours. Included were two, supercharged Alfa Romeo 8C 2300s, a model that had made its debut a couple of months previously at the Mille Miglia.

One of these, driven by entrant Francis Curzon, Earl Howe and former 'Bentley Boy', Sir Henry Birkin, took victory, after what *The Motor* magazine described as 'a wonderful race'. It was the first overall victory at Le Mans by any Italian car. Italy's ruler, Benito Mussolini sent his congratulations; 'Tim' Birkin declared himself unhappy about having to use an Italian car for his second Le Mans win.

The following year, Alfa Romeo went on to even greater success, with first and second places. Frenchman

● Not only did Matra dominate Alfa at Le Mans in 1972, but also Graham Hill, then in the twilight of his career, became the only man to win the Triple Crown of the Formula 1 World Championship, Indianapolis and Le Mans. *Motorsport Images*

To Europe

Chassis 002 sits below the René Herzog/Hans Heyer BMW 2800 CS in the Le Mans paddock. *The Revs Institute for Automotive Research*

Raymond Sommer won almost single handily after Luigi Chinetti was taken ill after just three hours at the wheel. It might be said that things got even better for 1933, with the 2.3-litre Alfa Romeos finishing first, second and third. The never-say-die Sommer was again the winner, partnered this time by Tazio Nuvolari, who was making his sole Le Mans appearance. It was the most exciting Le Mans finish to date, with a scant 10 seconds between the first two cars. The following year it came good for Chinetti, who had disputed that last-lap lead with Nuvolari in 1933. Chinetti was partnered by Sommer's compatriot, Le Mans debutant Philippe Étancelin, and theirs was the sole surviving Alfa, finishing ahead of a host of smaller machinery. (Chinetti would go on to become Ferrari's first agent in the USA and to run the famed North American Racing Team.)

Alfa Romeo had achieved four consecutive victories, making it the second most successful marque at Le Mans during the pre-World War II years. Its place in Le Mans history was assured, although it would never win the race again.

It was perhaps brave of Autodelta to enter its T33/TT/3s for Le Mans in 1972. It would be the penultimate year that Alfa Romeo contested the 24-hour race. The following season there would be just one of its cars present, a T33/TT/3 entered by the privateer Brescia Corse team, which was placed 15th. The 1972 entries may have been factory cars, but they were up against a formidable, as well as local, opponent, in the form of Matra.

'Suppose they built an unbeatable team of prototypes and nobody came to get beat,' ran the headline in *Road & Track* following Matra's domination of the 1972 race. That does seem a little unfair on Alfa Romeo, but the magazine did have a point. Alfa had simply swapped Ferrari for Matra. *Road & Track* observed that it had, 'changed from being the team Ferrari is faster than, to being the team Matra is faster than'.

Ray Hutton wrote in *Autocar*, 'The French team are something of an unknown quantity, as they have not raced a sportscar this year, but their cars can be expected to be quite a lot quicker than the V8 Alfa Romeos'.

The French do tend to win their own 24-hour race when the opposition is weak, and it has to be admitted that was the case in 1972. No native car had won the race since 1950, and Matra's season was concentrated on just the one event. Like Ferrari, it had taken advantage of the new rules to build a prototype using Formula 1 parts. Ferrari, having won all eight rounds of the World Championship so far, went the other way and abstained from Le Mans. It was said that engine-durability tests on a closed section of autostrada between Turin and Savona had not gone well.

At the beginning of the season, sportscar entrants had lobbied for the championship to be confined to 1,000km or six-hour events. Ferrari and Alfa Romeo said that their

The ill-fated Bonnier Lola crests the rise under the Dunlop Bridge.
Motorsport Images

Helmut Marko slips inside a Ligier JS2 at Le Mans. *The Revs Institute for Automotive Research*

cars would run no longer than this. Sebring and Le Mans went against their wishes, but the Italians turned up for the first of these. Both were also present for the Le Mans test day, but that was the last La Sarthe would see of Ferrari that year.

The circuit itself had been considerably modified, with a new section cutting out the dangerous White House corner and the Ford chicane re-designed. When June came, lined up against the Alfas were four Matra-Simcas, a pair of the fast but fragile Lola-Cosworth DFVs, and a host of ageing Porsche 908s. Autodelta entered three T33/TT/3s (although four had been on the original entry list, but then so had five Ferraris and two Mirages), all with large tail fins. One of the trio, that driven by Nino Vaccarella and Andrea de Adamich, featured a slightly lower flat rear deck, giving a less slippery shape than the more curvaceous tails fitted to the other Alfas. All the V8 engines had been given a 9,500rpm limit. Rolf Stommelen and Nanni Galli were lined up in one of the other cars, while Vic Elford was reunited with Helmut Marko and chassis 002, which had retained its yellow nose from the Targa Florio. It was an impressive pairing. The Austrian had won the previous year's Le Mans 24 Hours with a Porsche 917, while Vic had dominated the 1969 and 1970 events with such a car, only to retire. Toine Hezemans was initially on hand as reserve for all three cars, but went home to Holland on the Thursday before the race after a row with Carlo Chiti.

Autosport reckoned that Alfa Romeo's decision to compete was 'a truly courageous one'. Its credibility was now at rock bottom and, other than imposing the previously mentioned rev limit, nothing had, allegedly, been done to the engines to ensure that they lasted the distance.

Scrutineering took place at the beginning of the week. The minimum weight for the 3-litre prototypes was 650kg. The leading cars, including the three Alfas, all weighed in at about 720kg, with the Stommelen/Galli car the lightest at 714kg. Chiti had chosen Rolf to be 'the rabbit' at the start, a tactic used back then to force the pace in the hope of breaking the opposition, while other members of the team could sit back and watch what unfolded.

The first practice session of the week prior to the race featured occasional showers and damp patches on the track. This, perhaps, led to what would prove to be a false picture, with Stommelen's Alfa the quickest at the end of the day, after improvements had been made to the handling. He was followed on the time sheets by a Lola and a Matra, and then the two other Alfas. The second, this time dry, practice proved what everybody thought all along, the Matras were quickest. Both Matra and Alfa tried out a number of different tail sections during practice. Autodelta found that a down-swept tail gave an extra 700rpm on the straights, but led to instability. De Adamich declined to race with it, hence his car's use of the less-slippery rear. Elford, in 002, and Stommelen persevered with it.

Come the Saturday and, with a French victory expected, President Georges Pompidou was present as official starter, although it has to be said attendance was down; presumably the fact that the mighty Group 5 cars were missing outweighed the prospect of seeing a French win. Elford and Marko strolled through the grid, the former's overalls proving his allegiance to Alfa Romeo, those of the latter indicating that he was driving an Alfa rather than a BRM, but showing the Marlboro sponsorship of his Formula 1 team. Vic then donned his black, Union Flag-bedecked helmet, as he would be the start driver for 002.

The Matras responded to the President's presence by leading the race, filling the first three places, although Jean-Pierre Beltoise was quickly out when his car's electrics shorted out, causing a small fire. Jo Bonnier then proceeded to pass the two remaining Matra MS670s in his Lola. Behind these, and the older MS660, came the three Alfas. After about half an hour, rain closed up the field, and the second Bonnier-entered Lola (driven by Gérard Larrousse and Baron Hughes de Fierlandt) moved past this train of cars into the lead. The British 1–2 lasted just three laps before the Lola pair pitted. The Alfas, along with the Matras, stayed out for just over an hour. The stops saw a change in the lead, with Stommelen, first of the Alfas, lying second behind one of the Matras. The Elford/Marko T33/TT/3, chassis 002, was now in seventh place, just behind the third Alfa.

After two hours, the pattern of the race seemed to be established, with the quick Matras ahead of Stommelen, and Elford back in eighth having been lapped. Despite this, observed *Motoring News*'s Michael Cotton, Vic 'refused to be ruffled'. Following the second round of pit stops, which saw some tardy work by Matra, the lap charts went, in Cotton's words 'topsy-turvey for a while'. Galli had taken over from Stommelen and, thanks to Matra's sluggish stops, got away in the lead. It was, wrote Cotton, 'heartening to see an Alfa Romeo leading'.

Autodelta's problems began four laps later though, when Galli pitted with a sick-sounding engine. A dropped valve was suspected, but when he stopped again on the next lap, a faulty fuel pump was diagnosed. This was changed in a mere 12 minutes, but three laps had been lost and the Stommelen/Galli car had dropped back to seventh, although it was to move rapidly back up the field. The other two Alfas were now up to fourth and (002) fifth. The leading Lola ran into trouble, and by quarter distance the Autodelta cars were in third to fifth places, 002 being the sandwich. The two Matras, though, continued to lead the field.

As far as the French were concerned, all was now going to plan, their fortunes further enhanced in the night when the Alfas started suffering clutch problems. Chassis 002 and the Vaccarella/de Adamich car both had to have new units fitted. Just before midnight, all the prototypes stopped for new brake pads. Those on 002 proved difficult to remove, resulting in 10 minutes and three laps being lost, and Elford dropped back to fifth. Autodelta seemed to be the slickest team when it came to routine pit stops, but the pad changes were tending to average about seven minutes and the drivers were not amused.

At about this point, the older Matra had moved up

into third behind the MS670s. It seemed to be an uphill struggle for the Italian cars. To make matters worse, Elford, who was feeling ill, spun 002 and had to be helped from the car when he got back to the pits. At least it was felt that the three Alfas 'were running beautifully', even if they were falling back. 'The car was going OK, but we were struggling. It just was not as quick as the Ferraris,' recalls Vic. However, *Autosport*'s reporting team of Richard Feast and Robert Fearnall reckoned that up until about half distance, the Alfa team had 'proved quite able challengers'.

Dawn saw a chilly mist over La Sarthe and the failure of Vaccarella's clutch. A 10-minute pit stop could not get it working and he rejoined the race by starting the engine in gear, on the starter motor. Elford and Marko were also having clutch trouble with 002 and, soon after six o'clock, the latter pitted for a new one to be fitted. This took 37 minutes, during which time Vaccarella also came in again to have his clutch replaced. The woes continued less than two hours later when Elford spun 002 on the new section of the track, damaging the rear bodywork against a guardrail and losing another six minutes while a new tail was fitted.

At 8.25am, Jo Bonnier, veteran Formula 1 driver and winner of the 1959 Dutch Grand Prix, the first victory for a BRM at World Championship level, was heading into Indianapolis corner in his Lola. Ahead was the Ferrari Daytona of Florian Vetsch. The Swiss amateur, noticing the much quicker prototype approaching, swerved sufficiently violently to cause a spin. In the ensuing chaos, Bonnier's Lola hit either the Ferrari or a barrier and was launched over the Armco and into the trees. Coming up behind the pair was Elford in 002. 'I saw all of it happening just ahead of me, as if it were in slow motion. I could see Jo reckoning he was going to overtake the Ferrari as we went into the corner and I was thinking, "No, Jo don't do that. You are not going to be able to get by." Then, there was a great cloud of smoke and dust and I could see little else. I came out the other side and found the Ferrari sitting up against the edge of the road, burning. My first thought was that, as it was burning, Jo's car might be under the front of it as I had not seen it take off. As I stopped, a French television crew was making its way through the woods. I ran across the road. My first act was to look under the front of the car because I was convinced Jo's Lola was there. Then I thought that the driver of the burning Ferrari might still be inside, so I opened the door before I realised he was not there. He had already climbed out and run across the road. Both his hands had been burned so, instead of climbing over the guard rail he had fallen over it and was hidden from my sight.'

Bonnier died shortly after the crash. Although there would be more races to come for Vic, this accident would hasten his eventual retirement from driving. 'It was so unnecessary. Jo had been a good friend of mine.'

Elford's first thought was that he did not want to drive any more, so he headed back to the pits and said that he wanted to get out. He remembers, 'They told me to do one more lap and then come in again, and by then Helmut was all ready to get back into the car'.

About an hour after the crash, Marko stopped far out on the track, his replacement clutch having also failed. The hard-pressed Alfa mechanics found that the clutch had parted company from the flywheel. Chassis 002's career as a factory-run car was now over. Perhaps for the first time in his life, Elford was not upset that a car he had been driving had broken. He spent the afternoon just sitting around in the Alfa Romeo rest area before a solemn dinner that evening with the rest of the team. He then checked out of his hotel, not wanting to remain in Le Mans any longer and, as he later recalled, drove aimlessly south.

For the record, the Stommelen/Galli Alfa shortly went the same way, leaving the sister car of Vaccarella/de Adamich to survive a spin and, with new front bodywork, go on to finish fourth behind the two Matra MS670s and an elderly, refurbished Porsche 908. The Alfa finished 37 laps back from the winner. It just about summed up Autodelta's year. The team withdrew from the final two rounds of the World Championship, at Österreichring and Watkins Glen, to concentrate on the future. Alfa Romeo finished in second place, not far ahead of Porsche, in the 1972 World Championship for Makes, although the German marque had not even been running a factory team that year. Alfa Romeo scored 85 points, Porsche 66, while Ferrari was miles ahead, ending the season with 160 points.

Looking back on his season with the Alfa Romeo T33/TT/3, Vic Elford now reflects, 'The car was just not up to it, it just wasn't very nice. It felt heavy. It was nowhere near as flexible or malleable or as easy to drive as the Porsche 908/03, or even the 908/02 – they were great cars. Of course, it had nothing like the performance of the 917. The idea was great, but nothing worked really well. Autodelta wasn't up to it. None of us did very much testing. There just wasn't the money.'

● Elford out, Marko in. A pit stop for 002 at Le Mans in 1972. *The Revs Institute for Automotive Research*

11 June 1972 Le Mans 24 Hours, Le Mans, France
Round 9 World Championship for Makes

1	Henri Pescarolo (F)/Graham Hill (GB)	Matra-Simca MS670	344 laps
2	François Cevert (F)/Howden Ganley (NZ)	Matra-Simca MS670	334 laps
3	Reinhold Joest (D)/Michel Weber (D)/Mario Casoni (I)	Porsche 908 LH	325 laps
4	Andrea de Adamich (I)/Nino Vaccarella (I)	Alfa Romeo T33/TT/3	307 laps
5	Claude Ballot-Léna (F)/Jean-Claude Andruet (F)	Ferrari 365 GTB/4	306 laps
6	Sam Posey (USA)/Tony Adamowicz (USA)	Ferrari 365 GTB/4	304 laps
7	Mike Parkes (GB)/Jean-Louis Lafosse (F)/Jacques Cochet (CH)	Ferrari 365 GTB/4	302 laps
8	Derek Bell (GB)/Teddy Pilette (B)/Richard Bond (GB)	Ferrari 365 GTB/4	302 laps
9	Claude Buchet (F)/Jean-Pierre Jarier (F)	Ferrari 365 GTB/4	297 laps
10	Gerry Birrell (GB)/Claude Bourgoignie (B)	Ford Capri RS 2600	292 laps

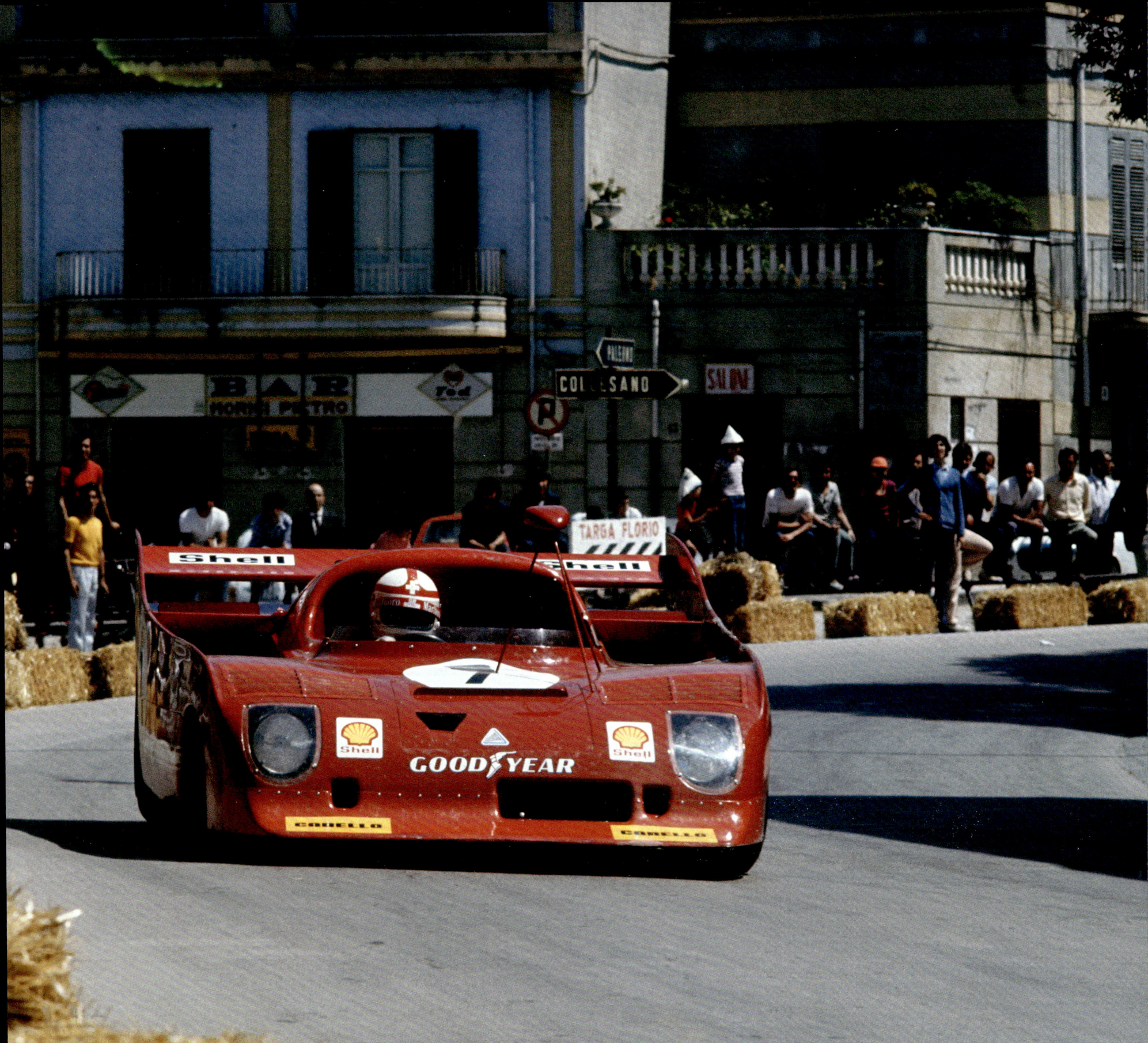

Chapter 6
The Alfas race on

- Autodelta ran a single V12-engined car at the 1973 Targa Florio for de Adamich and Stommelen. Once the two Ferraris had dropped out, it moved into a sizeable lead before crashing into a kilometre stone. A second car, to have been driven by 'Clay' Regazzoni (see here) and Carlo Facetti, failed to start after a practice accident. *Motorsport Images*

Autodelta's future plans depended upon a new flat-12 engine, which would power the T33/TT/12. Early-season non-appearances in 1973 gave it an almost mythical status. A car arrived at Spa-Francorchamps, but was crashed, resulting in its race debut being at the Targa Florio. There would be no finishes for the T33/TT/12 that year, and the Alfa Romeo flag had to be upheld by the privateer Brescia Corse team with its T33/TT/3. It has been said that this was chassis 002, although the subsequent history claimed for this particular machine makes it unlikely to have been the same car that was sold to Greek driver George Moschous a few years later, the paperwork for which stated that it was chassis number 002. (It may be that this thinking came about because of the similarity of the two cars' sponsorship liveries, particularly when seen in black and white photographs.)

Carlo Chiti was notorious for his lack of record keeping and cavalier attitude to chassis numbers. He should not be condemned for this, as chassis numbers meant little in the past, other than for travel documentation, and were frequently changed or falsified by many teams. However, it is said that deciding the identity of a Tipo 33 is perhaps more hazardous than is the case for most cars.

The Brescia Corse car performed solidly throughout the season – usually driven by Carlo Facetti and 'Pam' (whose real name was Marsilio Pasotti) – although it failed to start

- It has been suggested that the T33/TT/3 run by Brescia Corse, and seen here at Le Mans in 1973, may have been chassis 002. *Motorsport Images*

Alfa Romeo T33/TT/3 | 65

The Alfas race on

● By 1974, Autodelta had largely sorted the V12 engine. However, the T33/TT/12s were heavy and unreliable. An Alfa won the opening race of the World Championship for Makes at Monza but, from then on, every round fell to the Matras. The Italian marque did finish second and third at the Nürburgring with Carlos Reutemann/Rolf Stommelen and Carlo Facetti/Andrea de Adamich.
The Revs Institute for Automotive Research

The Alfas race on

the Targa Florio following a practice accident. It initially appeared – still in its Autodelta red livery – at Vallelunga for the 6 Hours, where it crashed. It would subsequently be painted in the team's blue and white colours, and it then remained in Italy to contest the Monza 1,000Kms, finishing fifth in this World Championship round.

The car then became the last Alfa Romeo ever to start the Le Mans 24 Hours, having qualified in 12th place. Its usual pair of drivers was joined on this occasion by Alfa tester, Teodoro Zeccoli, and a number of familiar Alfa factory faces were seen helping in the pits. The car climbed slowly up the leader board during the opening hours of the race. The 'old Alfa' was, observed *Autosport*, 'running like clockwork'. A fine performance during the night saw it hold third place for five hours – albeit eight laps behind the then-second-placed Matra – before gearbox, clutch and fuel-pump maladies dropped it back. Fifteenth place at the end was scant reward for the team's efforts. Next up came another World Championship race, the 1,000Kms at the Österreichring, in which the car finished seventh after a long stop for a leaking brake caliper. The final appearance of the car in Brescia Corse colours was at the Imola 500Kms, Carlo Facetti driving it to fourth place, its highest finish that year.

By 1974, the flat-12 engine was largely sorted, but the chassis was too heavy. Matra had now replaced Ferrari as the main opposition to the Alfas, but when all the French cars failed at Monza – the opening round of that year's World Championship – Autodelta enjoyed a clean sweep of the podium, the winners being Arturo Merzario and Mario Andretti. From then on, Matra won every round, and after Watkins Glen, demoralised, Autodelta withdrew from endurance racing for the rest of the year.

Alfa Romeo would win the World Championship for Makes eventually, but not with Autodelta running the show, and against negligible opposition. After winning the championship for two years running, Matra withdrew for 1975, and the calendar that year contained some locations one would not associate with a series originally intended to bring together classic endurance events. Willi Kauhsen, best known as a Porsche 917 tester and racer, quit the driving seat at the beginning of the year to take over the running of the T33/TT/12s from Autodelta. Derek Bell was signed up as one of the drivers. He recalls

that the first test that season was at Paul Ricard, where Alfa Romeo offloaded the cars and equipment. Bell was appalled with the preparation of the cars. Wheels were 'pointing in different directions' and rear wings were 'higher on one side than the other'. Writing in *Octane* magazine many years later, Bell remembered, 'Willi took on the project from Autodelta on the understanding that he would run the show and use his own highly drilled team'. Kauhsen would later recall that he had told Alfa he could only race its cars if he could use his own mechanics. 'I knew the Italians; they are not the right guys!' he said. 'What I have learnt at the Porsche factory, I will do with the Alfas.'

The cars were transformed, and won seven rounds of the nine-race World Championship, finishing at the top of the table with 140 points to Porsche's 98. After so

● The Brescia Corse-entered T33/TT/3 was the last Alfa Romeo to appear at the Le Mans 24 Hours. *The Revs Institute for Automotive Research*

The Alfas race on

- At last everything went right for the now Willi Kauhsen-run, Alfa Romeos in 1975, and they won the World Championship for Makes, albeit against limited opposition. Henri Pescarolo (seen here sitting in the car) and Derek Bell won the round at Watkins Glen. *Motorsport Images*

- By the mid-1970s, the World Championship for Makes had become a shadow of its former self, and a new World Sports Car Championship was introduced in 1976 to cater for the prototypes over shorter race distances. The Alfa Romeo T33/TT/12s won every round in 1977, albeit against lacklustre competition. Arturo Merzario, who had denied Autodelta at the 1972 Targa Florio, and Jean-Pierre Jarier won at Dijon. *Getty Images*

many years, Alfa Romeo had at last won what was once a coveted title, but it was a hollow victory. The cars had not even gone to Le Mans – seen as the ultimate prize – as the 24-hour race was not a round of the World Championship that year. Ironically, the Willi Kauhsen Racing Team (WKRT), which seemed to have salvaged the Tipo 33s from Autodelta's somewhat chaotic operations, then acquired an unfortunate reputation of its own as it moved into Formula 2 and then Formula 1.

The rules for the 1976 World Championship for Makes were radically re-written, with the major endurance races now to be contested by what were described as 'silhouette' cars. Something had to be done for the old two-seater prototypes, now known as Group 6, and a lacklustre World Sports Car Championship for shorter races, some requiring only one driver, was created for them. A new monocoque Alfa Romeo, the T33/SC/12, made just three appearances in the series during 1976, finishing once when it came second at Imola. The following year, Alfa Romeo and Autodelta returned to the series with serious intent and won all eight rounds with T33/TS/12s (a turbocharged version finished second at the Salzburgring). Given the nature of the competition, generally a pair of Toj-Cosworths and a few Italian-run Lolas, it did not mean much, particularly as this particular championship only lasted two years. Alfa Romeo was now starting to dabble in Formula 1, first with an engine for Brabham and then with its own, Autodelta-run cars, and so the Tipo 33s had raced for the last time as factory cars.

It had been a lot of effort for meagre results. There had been 2-litre class victories in the early years, and then the glorious blossoming of 1971, when Brands Hatch, the Targa Florio and Watkins Glen had all fallen to the T33/3s. The Autodelta-run cars only took one more classic endurance event against serious competition, the 1974 Monza 1,000Kms. True, there were the seven races in which the WKRT-run cars were victorious, and then the eight achieved by Autodelta in the swansong year, but by then the serious competition had left the playing field.

In addition to the factory efforts, older Tipo 33s were occasionally appearing in private hands around the world. One of them, recorded as 002 itself, had in 1975 made its way to Greece and, so, it is to the land of Achilles and Agamemnon that we must now make our way.

Part 3
On three continents

● Chassis 002 has become much travelled since its Autodelta days. Andrew Fletcher took it to Kyalami near Johannesburg, South Africa in 1989, where he finished runner-up on the aggregate time of two heats. *www.motoprint.co.za*

With the exception of the car entered by Brescia Corse, the Alfa Romeo T33/TT/3s graced the World Championship stage for just one season. Autodelta's focus was now on its 12-cylinder cars, and the 1972 models were redundant.

An example was to reappear three years later, Autodelta having been asked to make one available by Alfa Romeo's Greek importer. Carlo Chiti sent one of them to the Peloponnese, reluctantly it is thought, which he claimed was chassis 115.72.002, the car that finished second at the Targa Florio.

From that season onwards, this particular T33/TT/3 was to experience what can only be described as an eclectic career, competing on the primitive hill roads of Greece, making a brief appearance in Japan, racing in the shadow of Cape Town's Table Mountain, returning to Sicily to appear in a promotional film for an energy drinks company, and eventually becoming part of the European historic-car racing scene.

Its use of a V8 engine has, ironically, perhaps made it more suitable for its present role than the Ferrari 312PBs that were so superior to the Alfas Romeo T33/TT/3s s back in 1972, but whose 12-cylinder motors are challenging to maintain today. In 2018, the car was purchased by its current owner who, after a short season racing it with a two-valve engine (such a unit was fitted when it went to Greece), decided to revert to a full-race, four-valve unit, thus restoring 002 to the form in which Helmut Marko ensured its place in motor-racing folklore on that famous day in Sicily.

Chapter 7
Greek Odyssey

● The livery of 002 in Greece was similar to that of the Brescia Corse T33/TT/3 during the 1973 season, but substituting blue with red.
Courtesy Paul Moschous

With the end of the 1972 season, Alfa Romeo T33/TT/3 chassis 002's World Championship career came to an end. Its next destination was to be a far-from-obvious one – Greece. Said country's motorsport was relatively primitive, a few rich individuals racing over challenging, rugged, and sometimes pot-holed terrain. Racing cars tended to be used primarily for hillclimbing, a sport that could take advantage of Greece's mountainous nature. Any circuit racing mainly took place on airfields that might still be in use by the military, although there was also street racing in some areas, such as the island of Rhodes.

Alfa Romeo had a relatively strong presence in Greece thanks to its importer, Athens-based Motor Hellas, which had been competing with saloon and touring cars such as Alfasud Tis and an Alfetta GT. One of its drivers was Giorgos (George) Moschous, arguably the most accomplished Greek racer of the 1970s. Motor Hellas managing director, Perikles Fotiadis wrote to Autodelta's Carlo Chiti in December 1972 discussing a new car for the following year, and introducing him to Moschous who, he pointed out, would be driving it. He was, said Fotiadis, 'the best driver in Greece'.

Moschous had a private sponsor in the form of tobacco manufacturer Keranis (which supplied products under the Pallas and Delphoi brands). It seems that it was Keranis that facilitated the next step in George's career. The saloons that he was racing were run by Motor Hellas, however he was now about to move on to a 'pukka' sports-racing car, an Alfa Romeo T33/TT/3. There does, though, appear to have been reluctance on the part of Carlo Chiti to supply such a machine to Greece, and he is known to have been concerned about the state of the roads on which such a car would have to compete.

However, Fotiadis wrote to Chiti again in November 1974, apologising that he had not been able to visit Milan, due to sickness, but confirming 'the order of a car P33 for Mr Moschous, for delivery in February 1975,' asking Autodelta to prepare it and to send a list of the parts that would be required.

In April 1975, such a car was supplied for US$2,480, according to an invoice that was made out to one Arvanitakis Denis Panayote, described in another letter from Chiti to Fotiadis as 'your driver'. The actual amount was, as the invoice stated, 'valore ai soli fini dognali' – 'value for customs purposes', Chiti having decided to provide the car 'free as a symbolic amount', as Panayote recalls. The import tax, though, could have been 'huge', but there were a couple of ways around this. One was the ruling that a Greek student in a foreign country could bring in a car without paying any tax. Panayote fell into this category, and it was thus his name that appeared on the invoice, with the transfer being made at the Greek consulate in Milan. Panayote was no mean driver himself and already had an 'excellent relationship' with Chiti and with Alfa test driver Teodoro Zeccoli. Panayote drove the Alfa himself at the manufacturer's test track near the village of Balocco in Italy and, despite it not having the correct settings for the track, is said to have been fast. 'I could not explain what I wanted to change in the car's set-up, as I was driving it for the first time.'

Moschous also drove the car at Balocco. One of his sons, Paul, recalls that he set lap times 'almost equal to those of Alfa Romeo's test drivers at the time'. Another son, Manolis, states that he was actually quicker than regular tester Zeccoli. This was despite the fact that he did

● The invoice for 002 was made out to then student Arvanitakis Denis Panayote, so that the car could be brought into Greece without any tax being paid.
Courtesy Martin Halusa

Exceptional Cars

Greek Odyssey

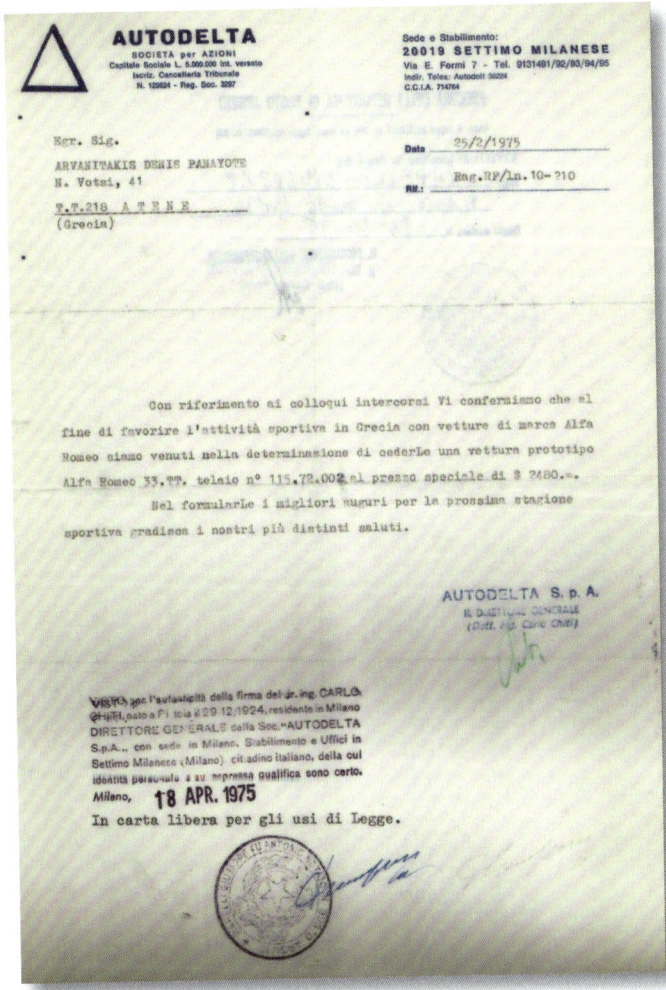

- Carlo Chiti's letter to Panayote states that the car is chassis number 115.72.002.
Courtesy Martin Halusa

- The local press welcomed the new Alfa Romeo T33/TT/3 to Greece.
Courtesy Paul Moschous

not know the track, the racing seat was too small, and the gear lever was sticking. A week later, says Paul, he 'was offered a contract by Chiti to join the works team in the sportscar championship, which he refused mostly for family and personal reasons'.

Manolis says that their father was asked if he would drive for Alfa Romeo in a 'more prestigious' race a week after the test, but turned this offer down as he was already committed to a race back in Greece at the Tatoi circuit. The Greek press reported that he had been offered 150,000 drachmai if he would compete in the event, which was at Monza. Moschous was well known as a man of his word. Journalist George Liveris, writing in the Greek national press at the time, referred to how the Italians had been surprised by Moschous's ability, and had tried to sign him 'for their team alongside Arturo Merzario, Henri Pescarolo and Derek Bell'.

Chiti did not give up easily. While Moschous was on the ferry returning to Greece, the Autodelta boss wrote to Fotiadis: 'I want you to convince Moschous to become Alfa Romeo's driver. I will offer him 7,500,000 drachma per annum with 25 per cent increase for next year. He will reside in Greece and he will race only when I call him.'

George was quoted as saying, 'Thousands of drivers expect this kind of dream proposition. Luck has helped me to be the one offered it. However, the reality is hard. Here in Greece we race 12 times a year, there we would be racing 12 times a month!' He stated that while his wife, Despina would allow him 'freedom of choice', his father would be firmly against him racing for the factory team. 'I feel very tied to my family and the Greek racing world.'

Paul Moschous and Arvanitakis confirm that the Alfa was, whatever it said on the invoice, the property of George Moschous, and there are letters from Keranis with details of the sponsorship that enabled him to buy it. Moschous had his own Alfa Romeo dealership and it was there that the car was stored until he sold it in the 1980s, and it was certainly Moschous who was then paid for it by its new British owners. Keranis had already been sponsoring Moschous for a couple of years when the idea came up to buy the T33/TT/3. Early mentions of it can be found in a letter dated 19 February, 1975. An agreement was made, whereby the car would be painted by Keranis – featuring its Pallas brand – and any changes to the colour scheme would need the cigarette company's prior approval. Moschous would receive 250,000 drachmai if he participated in eight or more races. This money would be increased to 400,000 drachmai if he also participated in the minimum of seven hillclimbs, with a further 100,000 drachmai should he win the Greek championship. An advance payment of 150,000 drachmai was to be provided to buy the car.

Documents still in existence say that the car acquired was chassis 115.72.002. Interestingly, the figure '2' seems to have been written in after most of the documents had been typed out and, almost certainly, using a different typewriter, although one contemporary document does refer to '002' without anything appearing to have been added or altered. Could it be that Chiti, who is thought to have 'muddied the waters' over chassis numbers, had been undecided about selling that specific car until the last minute?

Arvanitakis confirms that, as far as he is concerned, the chassis number is correct and that it was 002 that Chiti had always intended to sell to Greece. 'The car was fully original and accident-free with one problem,' he recalls. 'The injection pump was broken and it was replaced by a pump from an Alfa Romeo engine made for boats. This caused some issues, as boat engines were made to have a steady and flat function. They didn't have the specific

This photograph would indicate that Moschous competed with his T33/TT/3 at least once in its original Autodelta colours.
Courtesy Paul Moschous

spare part and it was not foreseen to manufacture one in the near future.'

There was one major change in the specification of the car since its Autodelta days. Perhaps it is not surprising that the car was not supplied with a full-race, factory engine. This had been replaced by a tuned, 3-litre, four-cam Alfa Romeo 'Montreal' V8. This is thought to have been one of the marine power units, derived from the 33 engine, that had made its aquatic-race debut in 2,500cc form in 1970, and had increased in size to 3-litres in 1972, which would explain Arvanitakis's memory. The engine was recorded as 'Montreal 2997cc no. 11-20-28'.

On 3 April 1975, Fotiadis corresponded with Chiti, following up on a telephone conversation in which he had asked for Teodoro Zeccoli and engineer Giovanni Marelli to be sent to Greece for the period 22–30 April, and to be present at the car's first race on 27 April. 'Messrs Zeccoli and Marelli will stay in Athens as Mr Moschous's guests, where they will have the opportunity to show some of their tips to our mechanics,' he wrote. Autodelta's Giovanni Arosio, who was also present for the car's Greek debut (he remembers the team breaking the oil pan when jacking up the rear), says that its transfer there must have had some importance to Autodelta or Alfa Romeo if Ing Marelli was there. Fotiadis also confirmed that there would be an official press presentation of the car at Motor Hellas Racing depot on 23 April.

Fotiadis wrote to Moschous on 11 April, informing him that the T33/TT/3 would be ready for delivery on 14 April, and was currently at the Autodelta garage with mechanics Doulamis and Massaccessi overlooking the final preparations. On 17 April the car left the port of Brindisi, bound for Greece.

Liveris's press report mentioned that the car had arrived on a ferryboat 'on Friday'. The combination of Moschous and the T33/TT/3 was, he said 'a marriage made in heaven'. It was felt that it would 'bring a breath of fresh air' into the races at Tatoi. Although the car arrived still in its Italian red Autodelta colours, it would be repainted in a different shade of red, its livery including a wide white central stripe with rounded corners on the nose, and white lower flanks. This new livery was reminiscent of the T33/TT/3 that had been privately raced by Brescia Corse in 1973, although that had been predominately blue rather than red.

Greek Odyssey

Reserved parking for 002.
Courtesy Paul Moschous

Although he would go on to be a successful rally driver with Datsun/Nissan, George Moschous's name still tends to be associated with Alfa Romeo.
Courtesy Paul Moschous

Moschous's arrangement with Motor Hellas for that season had two aspects. In saloon car racing he would drive the company's own Alfetta GT, while in sportscar competition he would use the T33/TT/3. While the latter was his property, Motor Hellas agreed to undertake the cost of preparing the car. All other expenses had to be managed by Moschous, although the importer would supply parts at cost price. This must have suited Moschous, who had his own Alfa dealership in the rich, northern suburbs of Athens.

Panos Diamantis, press officer of the Hellenic Motorsport Federation, records that, on 27 April, Moschous won first time out in the T33/TT/3, at the Tatoi airfield circuit, establishing a new record average speed, as well as a new lap record. He was to win again there on 30 November, bettering his lap record of April. Tatoi, still a military base, has continued as a race circuit up to the present day, albeit with a different configuration. One of Moschous's main rivals, another top Greek driver, the bearded Tasos Markouizos (or 'Iaveris' as he was better known) recalls how its bumpy nature made it a difficult track to race on. 'It sometimes felt more like rallying. There were almost zero safety measures, and trees lined the circuit, left and right.' The spectators were also close to the track. The races there were regarded as being in the top three most important motorsport events in Greece, alongside the Acropolis Rally and one of the hillclimbs. The attendance could be around 50,000 – an impressive figure.

Tatoi was also used as a stage of the Acropolis Rally. In its 1975 running, it was said that the only local man capable of staying with the international contingent was Alpine-Renault driver, Tasos Livieratos, or 'Siroco' as he was known. 'Iaveris' recalls that he, Moschous and Siroco were the leading three drivers in Greece at the time. He remembers that the three would compete everywhere they could in a whole variety of disciplines, although rallying was considered the true test, as circuit racing in Greece at the time was said to be less 'technical'.

There were three other victories that year for Moschous and the T33/TT/3, all on the Voula hillclimb near Athens, two in July and one in September.

'Iaveris' proudly recalls how, on other occasions, he was able to beat the Alfa with his homegrown special

Greek Odyssey

The airfield track at Tatoi was a far cry from the circuits that 002 had been used to racing on. *Courtesy Paul Moschous*

sports racer. Although the T33/TT/3 was the most potent car racing in Greece at the time, it has to be pointed out that it had been designed for endurance racing and was still equipped with lighting and fuel tanks suitable for long distances and, as such, was surely too heavy for a hillclimb car.

Manolis Moschous reckons that the T33/TT/3 never really worked well in Greece. It was awkward to maintain. It was also difficult to find appropriate tyres to suit the rim size, the team starting off with 15in and then switching to 13in. Perhaps it was not surprising that Chiti did not want the car to go to Greece in the first place. Manolis believes that Chiti was also unhappy that it would be used on the hillclimbs, with their additional strains, and not just on circuits.

Although the T33/TT/3 was considered a 'high-end' car when it arrived in Greece in 1975, there was no real surprise at its arrival. Over the previous two seasons, other teams had brought in prototypes, including a British-built GRD-Ford, which was driven by Makis Saliaris, who would later graduate to a Lola.

The tubular-framed, plywood-floored car driven by 'Iaveris' was initially based around an NSU engine. However, in 1975, this was replaced with a 2-litre Alfa Romeo power unit, originally a road-going engine, but tuned by the talented Christos Valasopoulos, or 'Boubis' as he was known, and the car was referred to as the Boubis-Alfa Romeo. The shape of the car seemed to change virtually every year, giving the eventual impression that it was a more modern car than the T33/TT/3, but it was a far cry from the factory-created and developed Alfa. Such was the nature of the competition that Moschous faced.

George Moschous won first time out with his T33/TT/3 at Tatoi. *Courtesy Paul Moschous*

Greek Odyssey

Greek Odyssey

● Contrasting Alfas: Motor Hellas made use of motorsport to promote the Italian brand in Greece. *Courtesy Paul Moschous*

● George Moschous, seen here racing 002 in wet conditions, was a natural racing driver who hated testing. *Courtesy Martin Halusa*

Quite what happened at the end of the T33/TT/3's first season in Greece is unclear, but there appears to have been a falling out between Moschous and Motor Hellas. In November 1975, Motor Hellas managing director Fotiadis wrote a brief letter to the driver stating the company was 'honestly sad that a co-operation of so many years is abruptly coming to an end. Motor Hellas can only accept your decision to stop this co-operation with regards to preparing your racing car.' Fotiadis then stated he hoped Moschous had made the right decision.

However, by February 1976, Motor Hellas was informing Moschous that the company would again undertake the preparation of the T33/TT/3 for hillclimbing 'and (hopefully, soon) circuit racing'. Motor Hellas would, once more, look after the preparation of the car as well as transport it to events and supply a mechanic. Parts and tyres would also be supplied as required, at cost price. Whatever problem had occurred in late 1975 seems to have been overcome.

The Alfa Romeo's victories in 1976 were confined to the hills, twice at Pititsa, setting new hill records there in July and November. It also won that year at the popular Dionysos hill and again at Voula, but it did not always go George's way. He was expected to win at an earlier Dionysos event, but was beaten by the Boubis-Alfa Romeo. It was said to be much simpler for him there in October, when he was competing against four other prototypes. By that stage it was felt that the T33/TT/3 had been made to work better on the hills, as Moschous won 'without even approaching the limits of his car'.

There was no Greek circuit-racing championship in 1976, for the first time in 18 years, but Moschous and the T33/TT/3 were able to claim the national hillclimb championship. Moschous repeated this feat with 002 in 1977 after having won at Voula, Hortiatis and twice on the hill at Ritsona, setting a new record there in July. The car was also seen on the island of Rhodes that season, competing in a hillclimb at Mandraki. By 1977 though, Alfa's Greek importer was experiencing financial problems, and so a halt was brought to its motorsport involvement. It transpired that the next time Alfa Romeo T33/TT/3 chassis 002 would be entered for competition was 13 years later… and in far-off Japan, where it was to fail during practice. It would be over two decades before it would actually race again.

George Moschous

Giorgos Moschous, in his youth an explosive footballer on the right wing, was born in Marousi in the north of Athens. He would remain there throughout his life.

His racing career dated back to 1966 when, then in his early 20s, he had entered a Volvo 122, belonging to his best friend's mother, for the Voula hillclimb. The lady was not even aware that the car was being raced, but George's second place, behind a Mini Cooper S, augured well for the future. Following the contest, the car was washed and returned to its owner. (George's father was unhappy at the thought of him racing, and so he then combined his names to form the pseudonym, 'Gemos'.)

For the remaining years of the 1960s, he raced mainly a Mini and then, in 1970, BMW's importer offered him a drive in a 2002. With this, he proved his worth, but mechanical failures meant that he missed out on the Greek championship by just a few points.

It was in 1972 that Moschous's involvement with Alfa Romeo commenced, a relationship that would last until 1976, although his name would remain associated with the marque for much longer. 'Alfa was really strong at this time,' recalls Moschous's son Paul, himself a former racing driver, 'and it was a disgrace for it to lose to BMW'. The threat from Alfa Romeo headquarters was that the importer's budget would be cut if the championship was not won the following year. Thus it was that Motor Hellas's CEO, Chronis Viconopoulos offered Moschous a drive with the team, initially piloting a GTAm. It was to be a successful partnership, although Moschous was indifferent to the technical aspects of the sport and was bored with testing. It has been said that his talent overcame this and, while the championship still evaded him, there were memorable performances at Tatoi, Voula and Ritsona. 'He had the ability to drive a car to the limit first time out without testing it,' says Paul. Moschous's other son, Manolis, another former

- George Moschous (centre) describes his car's handling to Perikles Fotiadis (left), the owner of Motor Hellas. Their mechanic, Doulamis, listens in. *Courtesy Paul Moschous*

- Moschous's initial experience with the Alfa Romeo brand was with a GTAm saloon car. *Courtesy Paul Moschous*

Greek Odyssey

racer, recalls an occasion when his father complained that a rally car was not handling properly. The mechanic simply washed the shock absorbers; Moschous then took the car out again and proclaimed that the handling had been vastly improved.

As described in the main text, Moschous acquired the Alfa Romeo T33/TT/3 that Carlo Chiti said was chassis number 002. 'I was a big fan of Moschous,' says Tasos Markouizos ('Iaveris'), one of his main rivals at the time. Before he started racing, 'Iaveris' had met George by chance in a bar. He now recalls that he was almost too embarrassed to speak to him, but later they became good friends. 'Iaveris' still feels that his Greek championship win in 1975 had far more meaning because Moschous was the runner-up. It was the opposite the following year. Their rivalry seems to have raised the level of the competition.

'Iaveris' remembers Moschous as being highly superstitious, 'so we used to mess around with him a lot, but he was a fun guy to be with in the pits'. He held George in the highest regard and still speaks well of him both as a person and as a racing driver. 'I loved him. He was a great driver.'

Moschous changed disciplines after his time with the T33/TT/3. 'The new thing in Greece was now rallying,' says Paul. In 1975 his father had finished seventh on the Acropolis Rally, driving an Alfetta GT for Motor Hellas, following this up with a fourth overall in 1976. Two years later, he would take the first of eight consecutive Greek Rally Championship titles. Now a Datsun (later Nissan) driver, he abandoned the circuits and hills to concentrate on rallying, winning 27 events. He was a regular competitor on the Acropolis, then a round of the World Rally Championship. While he was never again to match his fourth place in that event, he usually finished, scoring a fifth place, a couple of sixths and three eighths overall.

'In 1996, he retired to the Alfa Romeo dealership,' remembers Paul. Although a marble factory had been in his family's hands for three generations, George did not have much interest in it, and was more concerned with the eponymous dealership in Athens, which he continued to run until 2008. Despite the fact that he had competed in rallies for so many years with Nissan, it seems that his name was still associated with the Italian brand.

- An Alfa Romeo executive (far left) talks to the men behind the T33/TT/3 in Greece (left to right); George Moschous, Arvanitakis Denis Panayote, Chronis Viconopoulos and Perikles Fotiadis. *Courtesy Paul Moschous*

- Moschous moved on to rallying after his time with the T33/TT/3, initially driving an Alfetta GT with which he placed well in consecutive Acropolis Rallies. *Courtesy Paul Moschous*

Chapter 8
Home and abroad

Willie Tuckett took over 002 for the second event in the David Piper/Mike Knight-run ISP South African series, which took place near Cape Town at the Killarney circuit in 1998. *Patrick Beaumont Vermaak*

Sitting on the same grid at the 1972 BOAC 1,000Kms, albeit much further back than T33/TT/3 002, was the Chevron B19 of one Andrew Fletcher. The Scot had won his class at the previous year's race, sharing a B16 with Willie Tuckett. However, the latter was unable to compete at Brands Hatch in 1972, thanks to a driving ban, and future grand prix winner John Watson had been co-opted to share the little Cosworth FVC-powered car. In the event, the car's engine overheated before the Ulsterman got the chance to join the race.

When it came to motorsport, Andrew Fletcher had a pedigree that stretched back further than most. His grandfather, also called Andrew Fletcher, was probably the first, true Scottish racing driver. He is known to have defeated the great S F Edge in a 1903 match race on Southport sands, driving a 60hp Mercedes. A year later, he travelled to Nice and finished seventh in the Henri de Rothschild Cup, having competed against another Gordon Bennett Cup winner, and the first man to average over 100kph when setting the World Land Speed record, Camille Jenatzy. Other European events included the La Turbie hillclimb and the Circuit de Ardennes. There is no doubt that the wealthy Fletcher, a friend of the Hon Charles Rolls, was one of the true pioneers of the sport.

Andrew Fletcher's grandfather, said to have been Scotland's first true racing driver, poses in his 60hp Mercedes. He defeated Gordon Bennett Cup winner S F Edge with this car in a match race at the Southport Speed Trials in 1903. *Courtesy Graham Gauld*

Alfa Romeo T33/TT/3 | 83

Home and abroad

Perhaps the finest moment for the Fletcher/Tuckett partnership came with a dominant victory for their Chevron B19 in the 1973 Angolan Grand Prix. *Courtesy Andrew Fletcher/Willie Tuckett*

Chassis 002 on its arrival at Robin Smith's premises, following its purchase from Greece. Fletcher and Tuckett paid Smith £59,000 for the car and then spent a further £19–20,000 on restoration during 1987/88. *Courtesy Andrew Fletcher/Willie Tuckett*

It is recorded that he went to France, purchased six Bleriot aircraft, and imported them to England. 'After that we have no idea what happened,' says his grandson.

The younger Andrew Fletcher raced mainly Brabhams and Chevrons in the late 1960s and early 1970s. Swerving to avoid fellow Scot Jackie Stewart's car during a Formula 2 race at Snetterton in 1966, he became caught up in an accident, pulling all the tendons in one of his hands. He then moved on to sportscars, twice starting with his own, ex-Paul Hawkins, Ford GT40 in 1969, winning his class on the Doune hillclimb, for which the GT40 was totally unsuited. A full season with a Chevron B8 followed in 1970, Fletcher competing throughout Europe, with a fourth at Zolder his best result.

He joined up with Tuckett – who had previously raced an ex-works Le Mans Sprite and then a Gropa throughout Europe – for the first time at the beginning of 1971, the pair campaigning a Chevron B16 in the UK and on the continent. At the end of that season, Tuckett ran in six races in South Africa, sharing a Chevron B8 with Robert Grant. The B16 coupé was rebuilt into a B19 roadster for 1972, Fletcher and Tuckett sharing it for a programme of races around Europe, in which they invariably failed to finish. The Chevron did see the chequered flag once that year, with Fletcher finishing sixth in the European Championship 2-litre race at Silverstone.

Although there were one or two appearances in the Thundersports category during the mid-1980s, 1973 effectively saw the end of regular racing for both of them. Their penultimate appearance together in the B19 was in a two-hour race in Luanda in which they failed to finish. From there the pair went on to compete in the six-hour Angolan Grand Prix. 'This was one of our greatest victories,' remembers Willie. 'We won from pole position and were never headed. Andrew drove brilliantly.'

Fletcher also raced a Chevron B19 in a couple of races on the Iberian Peninsula that year. Both would, though, turn their hands to historic racing, and this is where our story re-starts. Veteran racers David Piper and Mike Knight had started organising races for historic sports cars, 'which sounded good fun,' recalls Fletcher. He decided to see if he could find their old Chevron, locating it in Canada. Having retrieved it, they had it built back into a B16 'because "Pipes" did not want an open-topped car in his series; it would have been too quick!' At the time of writing, Fletcher and Tuckett still own the car.

On hearing in the late 1980s that his friend and fellow Chevron racer, Robin Smith, was going to Greece, Andrew asked him to, 'look around for old cars. We have always had a collection of cars, and I thought that Greece might have something. I was really thinking of a road car.

'Within a couple of days he came up with this Alfa. I said, "Let's buy it" on the spot. It was not expensive but, when it got to the docks, Greek customs said we could not export it. It was of "national interest". So we took it to bits and had it sent to the UK in about six different packages! We then rebuilt it at Robin's place near Chepstow.' That car was the subject of this book, George Moschous's T33/TT/3 chassis 002, which Smith had found in the Greek driver's Alfa Romeo dealership. Fletcher remembers that it was covered in thick layers of dust. It was still in working condition, recalls Moschous's son Manolis, 'but not in tip-top shape'. It was now finished in full red livery and looking more as it had done when raced by Autodelta.

Laurence Jacobson, who also raced Chevrons, and had been part of a consortium with Smith and Les Cuthbertson that had owned Chevron Cars between 1980 and 1983, designed and built a honeycomb-section 'crash structure', which could be fitted to the front of the car for protection. Fletcher was impressed, as it could be bolted on and off and was not going to spoil the car in any way.

The car was first run up and down the runway at East Fortune aerodrome, near Edinburgh. The car seemed to be 'OK', even if the gearbox was not very good. Fletcher was pleased with the new purchase, 'It was light and nimble and it was good to be "outdoors" in an open-topped car after so long'.

The old circuit at Ingliston, in the grounds of the Royal Highland Showground, was also in the vicinity of Fletcher's Scottish base, so he then took it there for a minor sportscar race. He recalls it, 'would not rev. It had the wrong set-up. We had the wrong ignition system on it; it got to 5,000 revs and stopped.'

In late May of 1989, the car was transported to Donington Park, where Fletcher and Tuckett were due to race their Chevron B16. The idea seems to have been mainly to treat the occasion as a free practice session for the Alfa, although Tuckett, who was acclimatising himself to the car, did line up with it at the rear of the grid. It was a galling event for the team, as Andrew was up to third with the Chevron, having set fastest lap, before retiring with two laps to go. Eventually, the car was made to run well, 'and then,' as Fletcher recalls, 'David Piper came up with a trip to Japan'.

The Alfa Romeo was, thus, among the cars that were flown out in 1990 for the opening of the TI (Tanaka International) Aida circuit. 'It was a huge celebration,'

- Scottish motor racing historian, Graham Gauld took this photo of 002 shortly after its arrival in East Lothian, now painted in Alfa red. *Graham Gauld*

- Ingliston was near Andrew Fletcher's Scottish home, so it was there that he took 002 for his first race with the car, a minor sportscar contest. Ignition trouble meant that it did not feature in the results. *Courtesy Andrew Fletcher/ Willie Tuckett*

Home and abroad

recalls Fletcher, a host of veteran British drivers having been invited to take part in the private track's inaugural event, the Super Sports Festival. Fletcher and Tuckett both went to Japan, although the latter was to drive one of Piper's Ferraris. Unfortunately, during the first practice session the Alfa's crankshaft broke. The block was also damaged. To replace it, recalls Fletcher, 'We found a couple of Montreal engines, but they did not seem right'. Another Montreal engine was 'found lying about' in an engineering college and this appeared to be 'the right one'. The engine was rebuilt by Robin Smith and the car 'seemed to be going quite well'.

Fletcher, though, felt that the experience in Japan had rather put him off the Alfa. He still had his share in the Chevron, and was also driving some of David Piper's cars, including a Lola T70 and Ferrari P2, so he had no real need of the T33/TT/3 to compete in the various contests that Piper arranged. However, towards the end of 1998, Piper and Mike Knight organised a two-race series in South Africa for 'International Sports Prototypes'. The first of these, at Kyalami, the former Formula 1 track in Gauteng Province, was the only time that Fletcher was to finish a race in 002. The event was part of a Vodacom Festival of Motor Racing that featured 'Thoroughbred

- Tuckett and Fletcher saw an event at Donington Park in May 1989 more as a practice session, although the former was able to line up at the rear of the grid for the race. *Courtesy Andrew Fletcher/ Willie Tuckett*

- Chassis 002 went to Japan in 1990, but to no avail, as its crankshaft broke in practice. *Courtesy Andrew Fletcher/ Willie Tuckett*

Grand Prix' Formula 1 cars from the 1960s, 1970s and 1980s and two, 12-lap heats for the International Sports Prototypes, both during the afternoon of 6 December.

Local journalist Glen Smale described it as a 'hot Highveld day'. Over 22,500 spectators were there, many of them reminded of the great Kyalami Nine-Hour races that had taken place in the 1960s and 1970s. Smale was impressed by the 'commitment and resolve' of the South African drivers and by 'the glorious Alfa T33, driven by Andrew Fletcher'.

The drivers' briefing was early in the morning, but Andrew decided it was too early for him and missed it. The organisers duly punished him for enjoying his leisurely breakfast at the hotel by relegating him to the back of the grid.

At the start of the first heat, and using just first and second gears, Peter Hannen, in David Piper's green Porsche 917, blasted past the 2-litre Chevron B19-BDG of local star Gary Dunkerley to take the lead. Dunkerley then eased back past the 917, holding his own for a while until Hannen forced his way to the front again, then maintaining the lead until the end. According to *Motor Sport* magazine, Fletcher's T33/TT/3 and Carlos Barbot's Lola T70 led a 'spirited chase'.

It went wrong for Hannen in the second heat as he lost control of the 917 while lapping Chris Costa's Automa Special at Goodyear Corner. The result was a spin, which ended in the 917 T-boning Piper's Ferrari 365 P2. Both drivers emerged unhurt, while Dunkerley, who had been pushing the Porsche hard, went on to win the heat, as well as emerging as the victor on aggregate. Fletcher finished runner-up on aggregate time, ahead of Barbot and the Chevron B8 replica of local man Jonathan du Toit.

The Alfa then remained in South Africa over the Christmas period, while the British drivers returned home for the festive period. Tuckett, who had missed the Kyalami race, was no stranger to South Africa, as his wife, Alisa, was born there. It was he who then took over racing the car, which now carried sponsorship from Sabat Batteries, flying out from Heathrow on 16 February for the second, and last round of the series that was to take place five days later. The circus had now been moved to Cape Town and to Killarney circuit, from which the spectacular Table Mountain can easily be seen. Smale wrote that the almost sea-level altitude of

● Andrew Fletcher finds himself alongside Mike Knight's Matra-Simca MS650 and ahead of a couple of Lola T70s on the grid at Kyalami.
Tony Alves

● Andrew Fletcher finished second in one of the two heats of the International Sports Prototype event at Kyalami, South Africa in 1998.
Glen Smale

Peering under the engine cover in the pits at Killarney.
Patrick Beaumont Vermaak

Home and abroad

the track (compared with the almost 5,000ft/1,500m altitude of Kyalami) and its effect on performance meant frantic tuning during the practice sessions.

The front runners from Kyalami were missing, Dunkerley's Chevron having a damaged gearbox and the 917 of Hannen, a broken distributor drive. That left a trio of Lola T70 coupés as the favourites, along with the Matra MS650 of Michael Knight. The first heat saw Bill Wykeham's Lola fighting it out with the Matra before the latter was held up in traffic. Knight eventually fell back to third behind another of the Lolas, while in seventh at the end was Tuckett in the Alfa.

Nigel Hulme replaced Wykeham behind the wheel of the first-heat winning T70 for the second heat, and with the Matra suffering from gear-linkage problems, it was up to Willie to take on the Lolas. He recalls that he started some way back on the grid, but managed to get up to third place behind a couple of them (Hulme and Chris O'Neill). 'I must have come through the field quite quickly.' On his tail was another of the more powerful T70s, the earlier Spyder version of Colin Parry-Williams, and Willie knew that he needed a tow down the long straights if he was to remain ahead of it. Unable to keep up with the other Lolas to get that tow, he was overtaken towards the end of the race, finishing fourth behind the three Huntingdon-manufactured cars. 'I remember it was a great race,' he now says. Indeed, he recalls, 'It was a hell of a good weekend,' particularly the big barbecue that took place. 'I really enjoyed the Alfa. It was a lovely car to drive.'

The car made a couple more appearances in the mid-1990s, one at Silverstone, the other at Monza for another of David Piper's International Sports Prototype meetings, where it was to have been raced by Fletcher. He was delayed in getting to Italy, so Laurence Jacobson drove it in practice. 'I got there to be told the car had broken, so I went straight home again,' Andrew recalls.

It was also taken to the 1999 Goodwood Festival of Speed where 'it did a couple of very good runs'. On a further run, Fletcher spotted 'a splash of red' around a corner and nearly ran into a Ferrari that was being driven slowly up the hill. Andrew was understandably not amused and fell out with the organisers. There was one more run when the head gasket blew. 'A bad day,' recalls Fletcher. After that it was decided to give the engine

- Andrew Fletcher in the pits at Kyalami. The dangers of racing in Africa were not all obvious. Bill Wykeham, who won the first heat of the event at Killarney, recalls that, at their briefing, the drivers were warned about coming off on Turn 2, due to a possible lack of support from the marshals. It seemed that there was 'a bit of a snake problem'.
Johan Pretorious

- Silverstone could be a lonely place mid-week. Chassis 002 is seen testing there during early 1989. *Courtesy Andrew Fletcher/Willie Tuckett*

Home and abroad

a full rebuild, so it was sent to Langford Performance Engineering in Wellingborough, Northamptonshire. A dynamometer test sheet records that it then had a maximum output of 396bhp at 9,500rpm, not bad for a relatively low-revving endurance-racing power unit. However, neither Andrew nor Willie would experience this, Andrew's son, Henry, being the only member of either family who has driven it since.

Scottish motorsport journalist and author Graham Gauld, who was probably the first to photograph the car when it arrived from Greece, recalls that Andrew was a regular participant on the Ecurie Ecosse Tour that he has run since 1996. Around 2005, the tour was based at a hotel in Imola where, by coincidence, Andrea de Adamich was stopping on his way to Milan. Gauld invited him to dinner with the Tour people and, knowing that Fletcher still owned the T33/TT/3, placed the two together. 'They both had a great time talking about the car,' he remembers.

The car was offered at a Bonhams sale in Gstaad in 2007 (lot 234) with an estimate of between 860,000 and 960,000 Swiss francs (£358,000 and £400,000), but failed to sell following a highest bid of 760,000 Swiss francs. In 2008, it was decided to try and sell it through Duncan Hamilton Ltd, and there is a record of a Mauro Testi answering an advertisement on the 'Classic Cars for Sale' website and being told by Adrian Hamilton that the asking price was €375,000. However, there were no takers and the car was returned to Fletcher and Tuckett.

For some years the car had languished unused at the Fletchers' base near Edinburgh. However, with the 2010 Goodwood Festival of Speed, Andrew's son Henry saw a chance to enter this famed event himself for the first time. The theme that year was 'Viva Veloce – The Passion of Speed' or, to put it another way, a celebration of Italian motorsport and, in particular Alfa Romeo, which was celebrating its 100th anniversary that year. The car was far from being race-prepared, and a conservative rev limit had to be set. Still, Henry chose to compete with a timed run (many of the cars at the Festival are merely demonstrated, with no thought of beating anyone) and was pleased that the Alfa proved to be the second-fastest sports car, beaten only by a much more powerful Ferrari. He, perhaps naturally, now muses on what would have happened with a higher rev limit. The little Alfa was, he

- Henry Fletcher followed in his father, Andrew's footsteps by taking 002 up the Goodwood hill. *Author*

- It was Arturo Merzario (right) who kept Helmut Marko at bay in the 1972 Targa Florio. At the 2010 Goodwood Festival of Speed, he and Henry Fletcher posed with the car that he beat that day. *Courtesy Henry Fletcher*

recalls, 'excellent'. The event's Alfa Romeo theme also meant the presence of one of Autodelta's star drivers from the 1970s, Arturo Merzario, and a chance for the tall Henry to swap notes with a veteran Tipo 33 racer, even if the diminutive Italian had been with 'the opposition' in 1972, when he had, so famously and narrowly, beaten 002 to victory in the Targa Florio.

It was purely by chance that Goodwood weekend that Henry found himself on the same table as car collector and dealer, Franco Meiners. As Andrew Fletcher recalls, 'They got chatting and Franco, annoyingly, ended up buying it'. This is obviously something that he now very much regrets. 'I blame my son,' he says with a chuckle. 'It was a terrible mistake, I wish we hadn't done it.'

Chapter 9
Return to Sicily

A mistake by Andrew Fletcher or not, but, in May 2011, Alfa Romeo T33/TT/3 002 became the property of Monaco-based Franco Meiners. The latter recalls that, at Goodwood, he had 'looked over it carefully and seen how original it was'. He kept in touch with Henry Fletcher on his frequent business trips to London. 'Eventually, he called me back and said that we could do a deal.' Meiners then flew to East Lothian to meet Andrew and to examine the T33/TT/3.

The next time that Meiners saw it was at Neil Corns's premises in Finmere, Oxfordshire. This was near to Andrew Fletcher's other home in England, and close to where some of his Ferraris were maintained. Purely by chance, Willie Tuckett called in to see Andrew that day on his way to London, to be told that Henry and Franco were just down the road looking at the Alfa. Meiners was somewhat surprised to see Tuckett. The pair had known each other for, as Willie recalls, 'some considerable time,' through the European historic-racing scene and had shared drives in David Piper's Ferraris on a number of occasions. However, up to this point, Meiners had been completely unaware that Willie, who was to give him a lift back to Heathrow Airport that day, owned 50 per cent of 002.

'It came as a nice surprise,' remembers Meiners, 'It was like buying a car from an old friend. When you purchase a car it has to be a nice event. If you don't like the people you are buying it from, then you should not do so. The Fletchers are also real car enthusiasts, not people who are just selling cars for speculation.'

Once purchased, the car was then sent to historic race specialist Hall and Hall in Bourne, Lincolnshire, to check over such items as fuel tanks and safety belts, as Meiners wanted to go racing with it. That also meant inspecting critical components to ensure that they were in good condition and safe. The car had come with the two-valve Montreal power unit but, at the same time, Meiners purchased a four-valve, full-race engine, which Carlo Chiti had sold to his friend, Cuneo-based Giovanni Giordanengo, who was well known for his precise Ferrari replicas. Giordanengo had bought all the replica T33/2 'Daytona' and road-going Tipo 33 Stradale chassis that Chiti had been building for a Japanese collector. The prices had gone up, the cars had not been finished and Chiti had died, leaving Giordanengo to purchase many of the parts. These included the four-valve engine that Meiners was already aware of, having previously been told by Chiti about 'a special engine that he had made for the 33 in Greece'. It made use of a Spica fuel injection system, rather than a Lucas system, 'which Chiti had said would work well if you knew how to set it up'.

The engine was dismantled and rebuilt, as Meiners did not know if it had any mileage on it. 'When I then installed it in the car, it fitted perfectly. Behind the driver's seat

● Franco Meiners introduced 002 to the current form of historic racing. *Wouter Melissen*

● Franco Meiners travelled to Neil Corns's workshop in Northamptonshire to inspect his new purchase. *Courtesy Andrew Fletcher/Willie Tuckett*

Return to Sicily

was an aluminium panel. This panel was built for this engine, as the Spica injection at the front of the engine was practically into the cockpit. From this, I understood that this engine had been in this car. No other 33 has an aluminium panel like this', he says.

'If you look underneath the seat, you can see that, at a certain point, the chassis was cut and then extended by 10cm. The chassis were lengthened to make the cars easier to drive. You can see where the cars were cut, and the welding. I understood that this was car number two, and I knew that this was an early one.' (*Autosport* had reported that the cars had been 'lengthened a little bit' for Buenos Aires – see Chapter 4.)

One of Meiners's friends was the former Autodelta driver, Toine Hezemans. There was a certain aspect of the car, a special type of key, that had puzzled Meiners, and Hezemans said that this indicated the use of what has been described as the 'cheater tank'. This had been constructed with a false compartment to fool the scrutineers. Hall and Hall had changed the fuel tank, but Meiners had not looked inside the old one. Why should he have done? It was further proof that he had one of the 1972 works cars. (Although now removed from the car, the 'cheater tank' is today kept at Tim Samways Racing, where it is looked after for the current owner.)

- Shortly after its purchase by Franco Meiners, 002 was sent to Hall and Hall for inspection. *Hall and Hall*

- The gearbox removed at Hall and Hall's Bourne workshop. *Hall and Hall*

- Meiners had the engine dismantled and rebuilt. *Hall and Hall*

Now removed from the car, the evidence of the 'cheat tank' is stored at Tim Samways's north Oxfordshire workshop. *Author*

The only way Alfa Romeo could have beaten the quicker Ferraris that year would have been to make fewer pits stops and stay on the track for longer. 'Chiti was always cheating,' claims Meiners. The drivers had a key to open a vent at the end of the race, so that when the technical scrutineers checked the car, they would not suspect that the car could have been filled with more than the regulation 100 litres. In fact, the tanks had a capacity of 120 litres. This was not discovered by the officials at the time.

Meiners was also friendly with Alfa Romeo test driver Teodoro Zeccoli, who kept a diary of the cars that he tested. Prior to buying 002, Franco had looked at another T33/TT/3, which he noticed had an aluminium chassis. Zeccoli confirmed that two or three such chassis had been built in 1971, at least one into a complete car. However, unlike Porsche, Alfa Romeo did not have the technology to build such chassis successfully and, after the chassis failures on the prototype in 1971, it was decided not to race them. When Autodelta folded, there were still aluminium chassis in existence, which Meiners believes were used to build replica T33/TT/3s.

From the indications above, Meiners was convinced that he had a genuine factory T33/TT/3 from 1972, which he felt was chassis 002.

Return to Sicily

● Back on the roads of Sicily. This could be 1972, but it is 2014, with 002 reliving its most glorious achievement. *Jim Krantz*

● During 2012 and 2014, Chassis 002 raced at night for the first time since the 1972 Le Mans 24 Hours. Erik Maris (see here) shared the driving with the then-owner Franco Meiners at the Le Mans Classic. *Wouter Melissen*

Meiners raced 002 on a number of occasions, including at the 2012 and 2014 Le Mans Classic, often sharing the driving with 'a good friend of mine' Erik Maris. 'It was fantastically fast [at Le Mans]. It was an easy car for an amateur driver; the road holding was fantastic and the handling superb.' Other events included historic meetings, such as 2013 and 2014 Dix Mille Tours at Paul Ricard and the 2013 Imola Classic.

Meiners also received a surprise call from the energy-drink brand and Formula 1 manufacturer, Red Bull, to ask if the car could be used for a promotional event, filming for a video and also stills for its *The Red Bulletin* magazine. Thus, in late October 2014, 002 travelled back to Sicily. Helmut Marko was, by then, a significant figure in the Red Bull operation, and the company wished to celebrate on film, on the island where 002 had enjoyed its finest hour. There was another connection. Daniel Ricciardo, who had raced for Toro Rosso, Red Bull's second-string team, during 2012 and 2013, and who Marko had been mentoring, had moved up to the main Red Bull squad for 2014. Ricciardo's particular relevance to the story was that his father, Joe, had been born in Ficarra in the north of Sicily. The Australian would be returning to his roots. Ricciardo senior would later tell Meiners that, as far as he was concerned, the T33/TT/3 was a real racing car, not the things that his son was now racing. He was so happy that Daniel was able to drive the car… and in Sicily.

'It was a lot of fun,' recalls Meiners. 'Early one morning, I had to drive the car into Collesano. The road had been blocked for me. Inside the town was a famous 180-degree corner, a small straight and then a 90-degree corner. I had to do about 20 runs. A photographer was shooting photos from a ladder at a height of about 4m. He was almost in the middle of the road and I had to pass quite close to him. At first, with the sun coming up and the state of the goggles, it was difficult to see the road. On one run I saw a rat come out on one side of the road. If I had tried to avoid him, I would have hit the ladder. I had to squash the rat with one of the wheels!'

Meiners certainly had an excuse with those goggles. His helmet had been too modern, so an open-faced version had quickly been produced. However, Franco then protested that he did not have any goggles. The manager

Return to Sicily

● Daniel Ricciardo revelled in driving 002 through countryside once inhabited by his forebears. *Jim Krantz*

of the local museum duly appeared with a pair, said to have been worn by local hero Nino Vaccarella when he won the Targa Florio in 1971. 'They were all yellow, pitted from all the stones that had been thrown up. You could not see anything.'

Meiners drove the car in the morning, before Ricciardo arrived by private aeroplane, with Red Bull founder Dietrich Mateschitz, and took over for the afternoon. Out on the track, the photographers continued to risk life and limb in true Targa fashion. All that Ricciardo knew about the Targa Florio circuit was what he had seen in the Michael Keyser documentary film, *Speed Merchants*, that had brought to life the 1972 endurance-racing season. Reflecting on an incident recalled by Marko (see Chapter 5), he said, 'I expect to learn how to avoid donkeys while driving a racing car at 300kph'.

It was all very different to driving his Red Bull Formula 1 car. Hemmed in on either side by two 60-litre fuel tanks, with a steering wheel so tiny and flat that he likened the whole experience to being in a bumper car, Daniel pointed out the H-gate gear change. 'I've only ever used that type of gear shift in Formula Ford, and I wasn't all that good at it,' he said.

Ricciardo was obviously taken by the whole experience. 'I must ask why my grandparents left Sicily,' he said. 'Even if there wasn't a donkey on the course this time, I now know one thing. I want an historic racing car. It gives you a lot of satisfaction. You feel everything through the steering wheel, through the pedals. You know the car is old, but it still drives unbelievably. This car is a beast, it would have scared me a little bit.'

He also saw how passionate the locals were about racing. 'They noticed the car straight away. A few recognised me as well. They said they wanted me to be World Champion one day… but with Ferrari.'

From 2015 onwards, though, the car appeared less frequently in public. Much as he was enjoying 002, Meiners was also a dealer, and eventually decided that he wanted to move on to a Group 5 Lancia Beta Monte Carlo. With the Alfa working perfectly well, and the need to sort out problems with the Lancia, the T33/TT/3 was generally left alone. When it was taken out, Erik Maris drove it, while Meiners concentrated on the Lancia.

At this point, the current owner enters the picture, as Meiners recalls: 'He and I discussed the car for a long time. I suggested that he come to Italy and experience it at the Cremona circuit. He agreed that it was fantastic and eventually bought it.'

Chapter 10
A part of history

A collection of iconic racing cars – one from each of the first eight decades of the 20th century – does not seem a bad idea. It was certainly the dream of 115.72.002's present owner, Martin Halusa, who believes that this period is where the most interesting cars originated.

He was assisted in his search by former political journalist Nicola von Dönhoff, whose racecar-collector father, Hubertus, had founded the Nürburgring Oldtimer Grand Prix. When they came to select a car from the 1970s, they felt that they did not want to get into the ground-effect scene, and that a sportscar from the early part of the decade would be ideal. The choice seemed to be between a Ferrari 312PB and an Alfa Romeo T33. The former, although more iconic and successful in period, with its 12-cylinder engine, felt dauntingly difficult and expensive to run.

'We are not just collectors, but we also want to race our cars, and it seemed that the Alfa was an attractive balance between collectability and raceability. We liked the Alfa brand anyway. So, we went on a search,' said Halusa.

Initially, says von Dönhoff, the net included all 2- and 3-litre, monocoque and spaceframe Tipo 33s. 'In the end we decided to go for this car [115.72.002] because it has such a fantastic race history.'

Martin Halusa already owned an Alfa Romeo GTA, which was being looked after by marque specialist Alexander Furiani. The latter reckoned that the best T33/TT/3 was the one that belonged, at that stage, to Franco Meiners. Von Dönhoff contacted Meiners, to discover that the car was potentially for sale. The week prior to Christmas 2016, she and the current owner examined the car in Bergamo, where it was being kept. At that stage it was not in race condition, so Meiners then spent a few months preparing the car and, towards the

● Nicola von Dönhoff and Tim Samways with 002. *Martin Halusa*

● Chassis 002 sitting in Tim Samways's workshop early in 2020. *Author*

A part of history

- Tim Samways's Sporting and Historic Car Engineers took 002 back to its bare chassis. *Tim Samways*

- The gearbox has been overhauled by Samways's operation. *Tim Samways*

end of the following May, it was taken to the Cremona circuit, where it was driven by von Dönhoff, Halusa and his mechanic, Alex Ames.

'It was the most modern racing car that I had driven. I had expected that it would be a difficult car to handle but, as was explained to me later, these cars were made to be easy to drive so that the drivers could concentrate on the racing. It was like driving a kart; it did exactly what you wanted it to do. You look in a direction and it goes there. The brakes were incredible. I thought I was braking late, but I had to reaccelerate for the corner!' Both Halusa and von Dönhoff were taken by how far forward in the car they were sitting. 'It was really quite an experience,' says the latter.

The pair continued their research, von Dönhoff travelling to the USA to look at other T33/TT/3s. 'It enabled me to get a feel for what it exactly was that Franco Meiners had,' she says. 'It put it into perspective.' The decision was made that it was the right car to have, seemingly the one with the best recorded history and so, in December 2017, it changed hands, although it remained with Franco for some time before it could be transported to the UK.

It was decided to employ Oxfordshire-based Tim Samways Sporting & Historic Car Engineers to look after the car. 'Tim's is probably the shop with the most experience in Alfa T33/3s; he was taking care of two of them at the time. He did not have to go down an experience curve.'

Samways, who had come to the fore looking after Ferraris, had first run an Alfa Romeo Tipo 33, a T33/2, for Californian collector Peter Read. This was followed by a T33/TT/3, which Read drove with endurance-racing legend Brian Redman at the 2012 Le Mans Classic. Read eventually sold this car, but Samways would continue working on Tipo 33s when Alexander Rittweger bought a T33/TT/3 and a T33/TT/12. 'Alfas are not normal cars to buy,' Samways observes. 'You have really got to want one.' Read then came back into the picture when an old friend of his, Gianluca Rattazzi said that he, too, wanted an Alfa Romeo. The result was the T33/3 that Samways now runs on Rattazzi's behalf. Rattazzi originally teamed up with Tipo 33 veteran Nanni Galli to race this car, but when the latter sadly became too ill to compete, he turned to serial Le Mans winner Emanuele Pirro to be his co-driver.

● Niklas (kneeling) and Lukas Halusa with 002 at Silverstone. *Martin Halusa*

Samways's operation took 115.72.002 back to its bare chassis, and a mechanical overhaul was carried out to ensure reliability and safety. The gearbox was refurbished, and a higher roll hoop was fitted to comply with current regulations. The bodywork was in 1972 style and featured an open, slatted rear, and front splitters. These had to be changed, as the car needed to be in 1971 specification to ensure FIA approval to run in the desired class. The fuel tanks were also replaced with fresh bag tanks and a new casing.

Both the Montreal and four-valve engines had been included with the car, and it was initially decided to race with the former. This was then used throughout the 2019 season, while work was carried out on the four-valve unit the following year, as Halusa wanted this engine to be completely refurbished before he used it,

A part of history

- Lukas Halusa in the rain at the Circuit de Barcelona-Catalunya. The yellow nose, decals and the number 17 mirror the car as it was at the 1972 Le Mans 24 Hours. *Wouter Melissen*

- Alfa Romeo T33/TT/3 002 leads an eclectic field at the Espiritu de Montjuic during 2019. *Wouter Melissen*

remarking: 'Then we can start racing it seriously'. As far as Samways is concerned, the four-valve engine is 'an Italian [Cosworth] DFV which never had the same development'. He also points out that for Autodelta, as for Ferrari, the engine was the most important aspect of the car. The Montreal unit was also rebuilt during 2020, which has resulted in an increase in its power.

Initially, 002 was taken to the Anglesey Circuit in Wales. Problems were found with the wiring – Samways describes the harness as having been 'scruffy' – and so a replacement loom was made before the new owner could start competing with the car.

The 2019 races were seen more as a long test session to assess the weaknesses of the car and to determine the points that Samways should focus on. Five meetings were entered for a total of seven races, most of which, as Halusa admits, 'We did not finish'. He continued, 'It had not been raced for many years and the car was not in perfect condition. The engine was also not up to it; we did not have a lot of power.'

The first races, part of the Peter Auto Classic Endurance Racing series, took place on 7 July at the Circuit de Barcelona-Catalunya, the car still fitted with its 1972 bodywork. Neither Martin, nor his son, Lukas were able to finish their respective races. It rained during practice, but Samways recalls how good Lukas was, despite the conditions.

'The only times it ever worked were at the Silverstone Classic meeting and at the Nürburgring Oldtimer Grand Prix,' says Martin reflectively. At the former, Lukas and

A part of history

Alfa Romeo T33/TT/3

A part of history

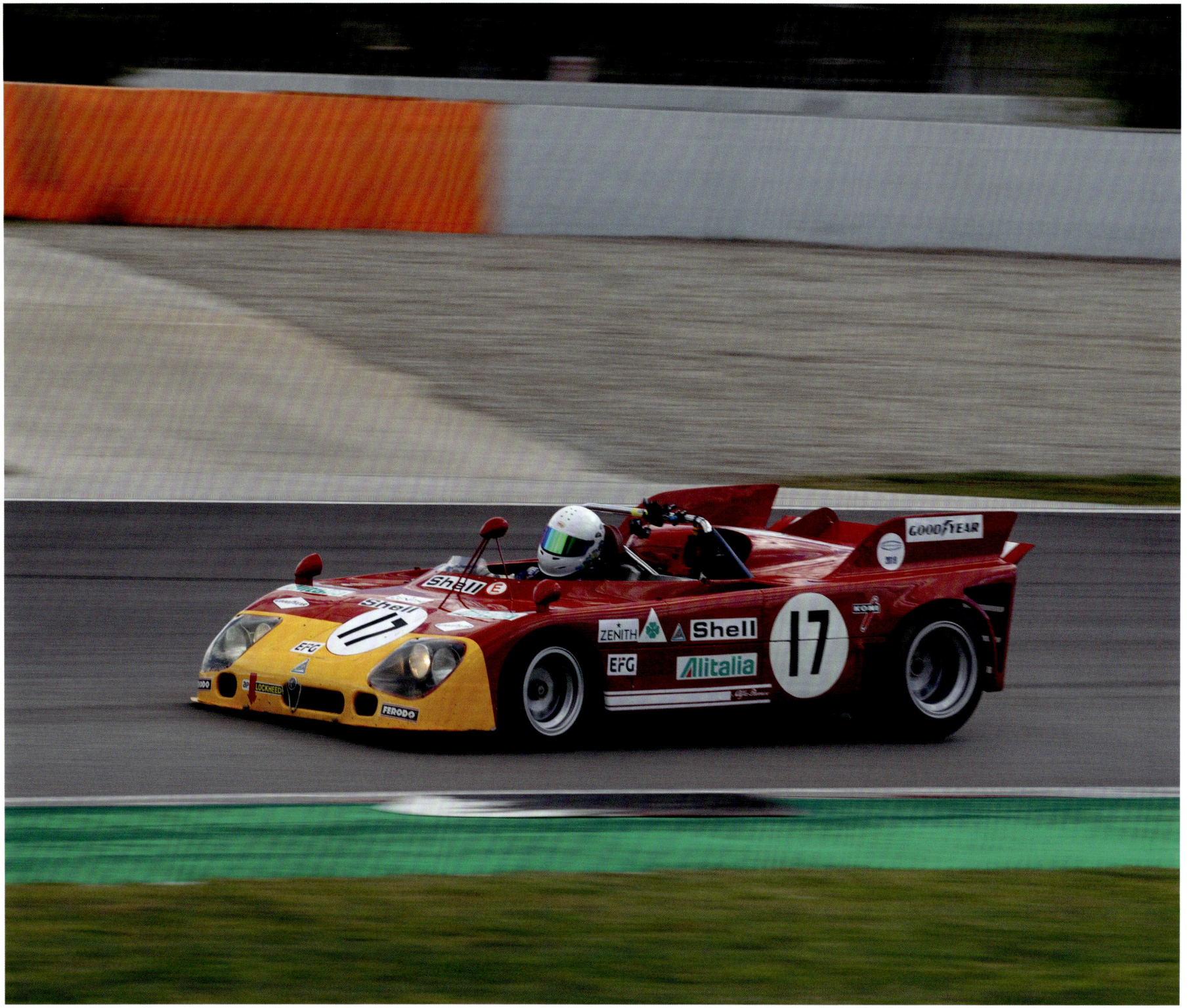

A part of history

○ Lukas Halusa races 002. 'These are family events,' remarks his father, Martin. *Wouter Melissen*

his brother, Niklas, finished 11th, while at the latter, their father, who according to Samways seemed to be thoroughly enjoying himself, came in 12th. Both these events were rounds of the FIA Masters Historic Sports Car Championship, as was a wet Spa Six Hours. The brothers were again at the wheel in Belgium but, once more, the car failed to finish. Finally, there were two races at the Paul Ricard circuit in southern France, in October, one with the owner behind the wheel, the other with Lukas and, yes, the car retired, although the latter had, according to Samways, 'driven his heart out in qualifying'. The last-minute appearance of heavy rain had meant that he was forced to start on the wrong tyres and had to pit straight away, rejoining a lap adrift. From then on, he matched the speed of the front-runners before retiring with water in the electrics. The feedback, though, had been invaluable.

Martin explains: 'The truth is that I am more of a collector who likes to drive the car. I did not start racing until I was in my mid-50s. My boys are in their 20s and both of them have become pretty competent.' Niklas won the Kinrara Trophy at the 2018 Goodwood Revival, sharing his father's unique Ferrari 250 GT SWB 'Breadvan' with Emanuele Pirro.

Lukas has won with that car at the 2018 Le Mans Classic, while there was a brace of victories for Lukas at Imola two years before and a shared victory for them at Monza in 2015. Martin continues: 'They have become good at not crashing. There are other owners who are wary of letting their children drive their valuable cars. I love it; these are family events. I could not think of a better way of spending a weekend than racing with my boys. I get much more pleasure from them doing well than any success of my own.

'I look at my cars like an art collection. In the Alfa Romeo T33/TT/3 I own an important part of automotive history. It has a fabulous race history and it represents the pinnacle of technical ambition and skill, as well as racing passion, for that era.'

○ The Halusa family has had success with the unique Ferrari 250 GT SWB 'Breadvan' seen here at Goodwood. *Jeff Bloxham*

Chapter 11
Photo gallery
Photography by John Colley

Style was beginning to be overcome by function for endurance racers by the time of the Alfa Romeo T33/TT/3. The car's detractors said that it looked like a red Porsche 908/03 when it first appeared. Perhaps that is appropriate: the look of the first 908 spyder in some ways harked back to the past. The very different lines of the later 908/3 pointed to the future.

This was also a time for spyders. There had been a thinly veiled pretence that the Group 5 cars, which had ruled for the past two seasons, were production sportscars and with the regulations specifying windscreens, these cars had been coupés. With no such requirement and no weight restriction for Group 6, the spyder body became, as Ian Bamsey pointed out in *The Anatomy & Development of the Sports Prototype Racing Car*, 'standard wear, even at Le Mans'.

In one way, the T33/TT/3 did connect with the past, in that while racing cars were at the time moving towards monocoque construction, it featured a tubular spaceframe. The prototype made use of an aluminium frame, but this had been changed to a more robust, heavier steel frame by the time the cars first raced in 1972.

These evocative studio photos, taken by John Colley, take us back to when the 3-litre spyders ruled the classic races.

● Pristine, and beautifully restored at Tim Samways's Oxfordshire workshop, Alfa Romeo T33/TT/3 chassis 115.72.002 displays its classic spyder lines.

● The T33/TT/3 featured a shorter wheelbase than its predecessors, with the driver sitting well forwards. The oil tank for the T33/TT/3's dry-sump lubrication system is located ahead of the radiator, within the cooling duct on the left-hand side of the car. The large fins on the rear bodywork were added part-way through the European leg of the season.

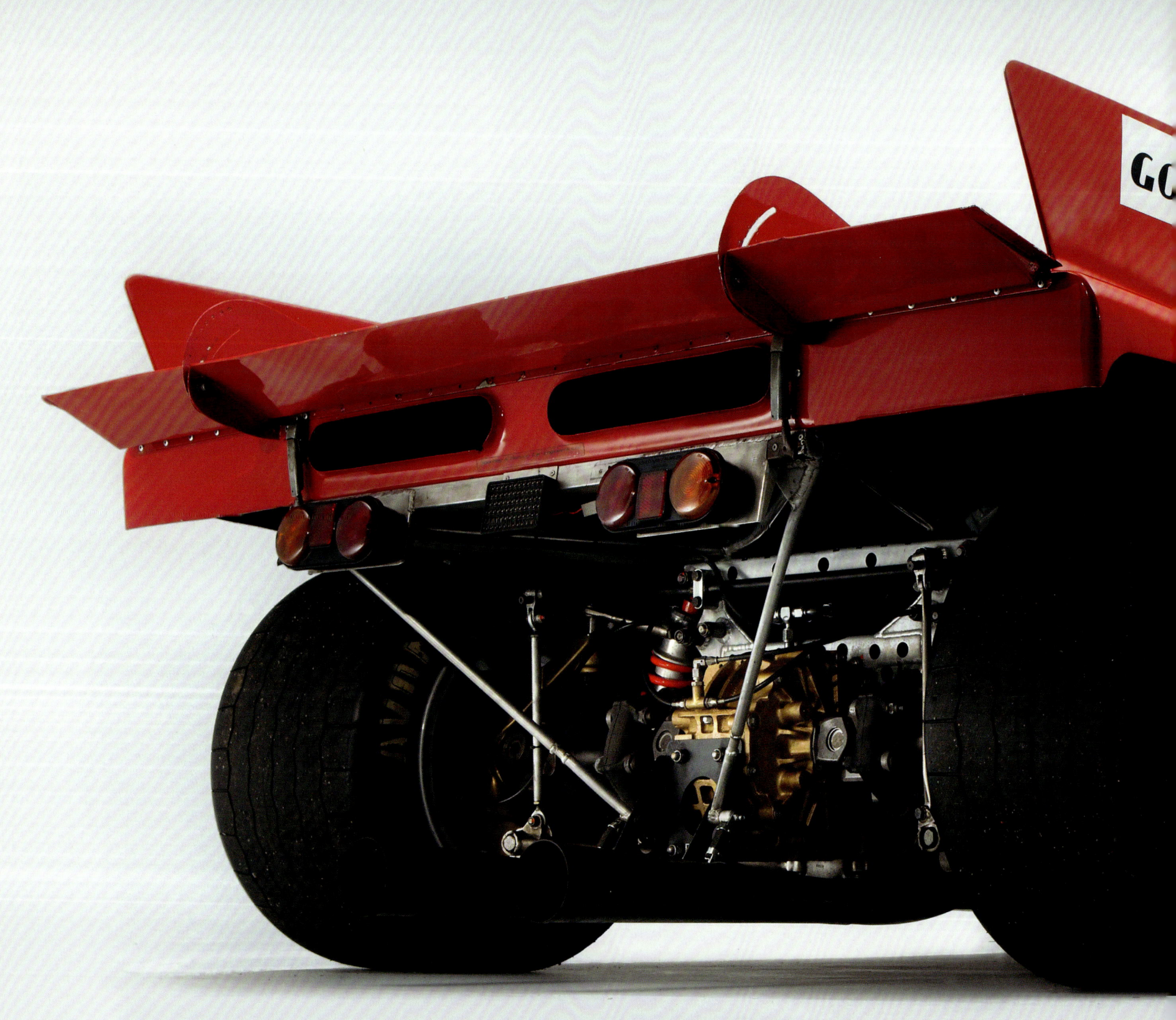

- All the T33/TT/3s that were raced featured a tubular steel spaceframe. The chassis identification plate is positioned towards the front right-hand side of the frame. To aid the shortening of the wheelbase, and weight distribution, a new five-speed gearbox was developed for the T33/TT/3, located between the engine and rear axle, rather than behind the latter.

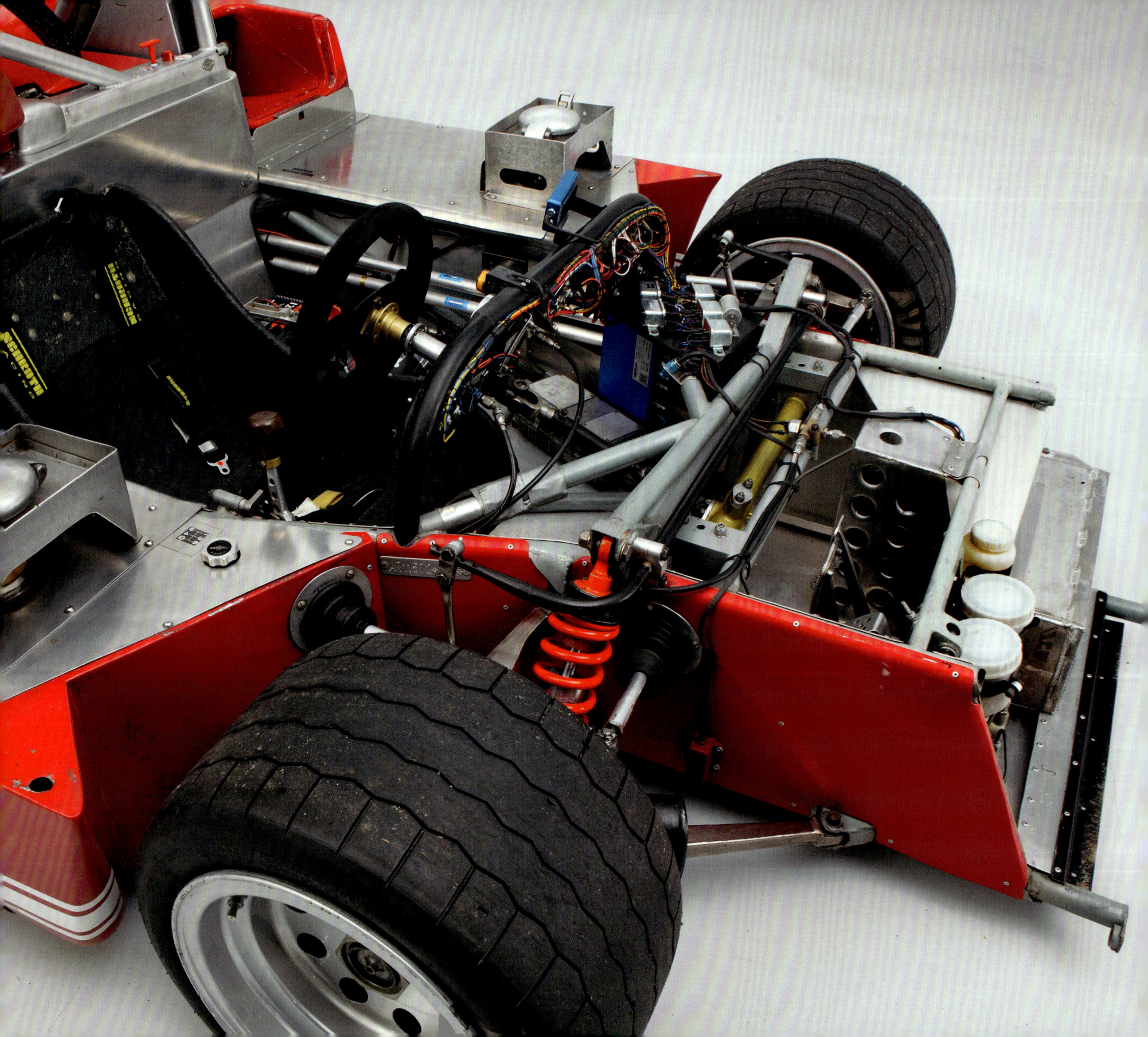

- As the proposed flat-12 engine was still not ready, Autodelta had to make use of the well-proven V8 unit for another year in 1972. The engine had been further developed, with redesigned cylinder heads, and 440bhp was being claimed. The five-speed gearbox has a conventional selector-gate pattern, with the brake-bias adjuster fitted alongside the gearlever.

124 | Exceptional Cars

Acknowledgements

David Abrahams
Tony Alves
Patrick Beaumont Vermaak
Jeff Bloxham
George Boron
Peter Collins
Andrea de Adamich
Panos Diamantis
Vic Elford
Andrew Fletcher
Henry Fletcher
David Freestone
Graham Gauld
Christopher Gregory
Martin Halusa
Steve Humble
Laurence Jacobsen
Tim Jacobsen
Achilleas Kalogirou
Mike Knight
Jim Krantz
Andrew Marriott
Tasos Markouizos
Ed McDonough
Franco Meiners
Wouter Melissen
Paul Moschous
Manolis Moschous
Doug Nye
Arvanitakis Denis Panayote
Dimitris Papadoulos
David Pearson
Liz and David Piper
Johan Pretorious
Ian Rankin
Tim Samways
Claudy Schmitz
John Stroud
Gerald Swan
Stephanie Sykes-Dunmore
Glen Smale
Jane Tagford
Tommy Thomson
Willie Tuckett
Paul Vesty
Grant Viljoen
Nicola von Dönhoff
Richard Wagstaff
Margaret Webb
Tim Wright
Bill Wykeham
Nicholas Zalmas
Ulrich Zensen

Bibliography

Books

Alfa Romeo The Legend Revived by David Styles, Dalton Watson 1989
Alfa Romeo Tipo 33 by Peter Collins and Ed McDonough, Veloce Publishing 2005
Alfa Romeo Tipo 6C by Angela Cherrett, Haynes Publishing 1989
Autocourse 1972-73 edited by Mike Kettlewell, Haymarket Publishing 1972
Autocourse 1973-74 edited by Mike Kettlewell, Haymarket Publishing 1973
Autodelta: Alfa Romeo Racing 1963-1983 by Maurizio Tabucchi, Giorgio Nada Editore
Chevron, the Derek Bennett Story by David Gordon, Patrick Stephens Ltd 1991
Daytona 24 Hours The Definitive History of America's Great Endurance Race by J J O'Malley, David Bull Publishing 2003
Directory of Classic Prototypes and Grand Touring Cars by Anthony Pritchard, Aston Publications 1988
Famous Racing Cars by David Hodges, Temple Press 1962
Ferrari 312 & 512 Sports Racing Cars by Ian Bamsey, Haynes Publishing 1986
Ferrari 312P and 312PB by Ed McDonough and Peter Collins, Veloce Publishing 2009
Grand Prix Cars 1945-65 by Mike Lawrence, Aston Publications 1989
Italian Racing Red by Karl Ludvigsen, Ian Allan 2008
Le Mans by Anders Ditlev Clausager, Arthur Barker 1982
Le Mans: The Ford and Matra Years 1966-1974 by various, Brooklands Books 1979
Le Mans: The Official History of the World's Greatest Race 1970-79 by Quentin Spurring, Evro Publishing 2014
Scottish Motor Racing and Drivers by Graham Gauld, Havelock Publishing 2004
Sebring: The Official History of America's Great Sports Car Race by Ken Breslauer, David Bull Publishing 1995
Targa Florio, Seventy Epic Years of Motor Racing by David Owen, Haynes Publishing 1979
Targa Florio: The Porsche and Ferrari Years, 1965-73 by Various, Brooklands Books 1999
The Alfa Romeo Tradition by Griffith Borgeson, Haynes Publishing 1990
The Anatomy & Development of the Sports Prototype Racing Car by Ian Bamsey, Haynes Publishing 1991
The World's Racing Cars by M L Twite, Macdonald 1964
Time and Two Seats by János Wimpffen, Motorsport Research Group 1999
Vic Elford: Reflections on a Golden Era in Motorsports by Vic Elford, David Bull Publishing 2008
World Encyclopaedia of Racing Drivers by Peter Higham, Haynes Publishing 2013

Magazines

Autocar
Autosport
Autosport & Classics
Competition Press & Autoweek
Modern Motor
Motor
Motoring News
Motor Sport
Road & Track

DVD

The Speed Merchants produced by Michael Keyser, Duke Marketing

Index

Abarth 31, 45, 52
Acropolis Rally 76, 81
Adamich, Andrea de 19, 22, 25, 27, 32, 34, 35, 36, 37, 42, 45, 46, 47, 48, 50, 52, 53, 54, 55, 56, 61, 62, 65, 66, 91
Alberti, Giovanni 32, 35
Alfa Romeo
   158 8, 13
   158 'Alfetta' 12
   158 'Alfetta' GT 72, 76, 81
   159 8, 13
   6C 13, 14
   6C 2500 Competizione 14
   6C 3000 Competizione Maggiorate 14, 18
   8C 8, 10, 14, 57
   8C 2300 57
   8C 2900 B Berlinetta Touring 14
   C52 'Disco Volante' 14, 18
   Giulia 16
   Giulia TZ2 18
   GT 16
   GTA 16, 100
   GTAm 18
   P.1 10
   P.2 10
   Tipo 33 6, 8, 16-21, 22, 42, 47, 48, 53, 65, 68, 91, 92, 100, 102
   Tipo B Monoposto 10, 12
   T33/TT/12 52, 65, 66, 67, 102
   T33/2 'Daytona' 92
   T33/2 16, 17, 19, 21, 53, 102
   T33/3 21, 22, 27, 32, 35, 36, 37, 47, 53
   T33/SC/12 68
   TZ 16, 18
   TZ2 GT 18
Andretti, Mario 35, 36, 37, 41, 45, 46, 67
Ascari, Alberto 10
Ascari, Antonio 10
Auto Union 8, 10, 12
Autodelta 6, 16, 18, 21, 22, 24, 25, 27, 31, 32, 33, 34, 35, 36, 37, 38, 39, 41, 42, 45, 47, 48, 50, 53, 54, 55, 56, 58, 61, 64, 65, 66, 67, 68, 71, 72, 74, 75, 85, 91, 94, 95, 104, 123
Automobili Turismo e Sport (ATS) 18
Autosport 25, 31, 32, 35, 36, 38, 41, 42, 45, 48, 52, 54, 61, 62, 67, 94
Baghetti, Giancarlo 18
Bagration, Jorge de 31, 35
Balocco test track 16, 31, 72
Bell, Derek 55, 56, 62, 67, 68, 74
Bianchi, Lucien 19, 53
Biondetti, Clemente 14
Birkin, Sir Henry 14, 57
BMW 80
   2800 CS 58
Bonnier, Jo 35, 39, 41, 56, 59, 61, 62
Bornigia, Mario and Giancarlo 14
Boubis 77, 79
Bourgoignie, Claude 21, 62
Brabham 18, 47, 53, 68, 84
Brabham-Alfa Romeo BT23 53
Brands Hatch 29, 47, 48, 68, 83
BOAC 1,000Kms 22, 42-46, 83
Brescia Corse 58, 65, 67, 71, 72, 75
Bridges, John 35, 56
Brilli-Peri, Gaston 10
Brivio, Antonio 14, 49
BRM 39, 41, 61, 62
   P167 48
Buenos Aires 1,000Kms 31, 32, 34, 35, 36, 42, 94
Campari, Giuseppe 10, 14
Casoni, Mario 20, 55, 62
Chevrolet 48
   Camaro 41
   Corvette 37, 41
Chevron 84, 85, 86, 87
   B8 84, 87
   B16 22, 83, 84, 85
   B19 35, 44, 46, 51, 55, 83, 84
   B19/21 45, 56
   B19-BDG 87, 89
Chinetti, Luigi 10, 58
Chinetti, Luigi Jr 41
Chiti, Carlo 6, 16, 18, 21, 22, 25, 27, 31, 32, 35, 38, 48, 50, 53, 54, 61, 65, 71, 72, 74, 75, 77, 81, 92, 95
Christos Valasopoulos *see* Boubis
Commission Sportive Internationale (CSI) 29
Cooper 21, 33
Côte de Fléron hillclimb 16
Cotton, Michael 25, 35, 42, 45, 48, 61
Cremona circuit 98, 102
Datsun 76, 81
Daytona 24 Hours 19, 31, 33, 35-37, 38, 41, 62
Dechent, Hans-Dieter 31, 33, 39
Dönhoff, Nicola von 100, 102
Doulamis 75, 80
Dunkerley, Gary 87, 89
Ecurie Bonnier 35, 42, 61
Edwards, Guy 45, 46
Elford, Vic 25, 27, 31, 32, 33, 34, 35, 36, 37, 38, 39, 41, 42, 45, 46, 47, 48, 50, 53, 54, 55, 56, 57, 60, 61, 62
European Touring Car Championship (ETCC) 18
Facetti, Carlo 20, 25, 31, 32, 35, 65, 66, 67
Fangio, Juan Manuel 13, 14
Farina, Giuseppe 13
Feast, Richard 45, 62
Fernandez, Juan 31, 35
Ferrari 6, 8, 10, 12, 13, 18, 22, 27, 29, 31, 32, 34, 35, 36, 37, 38, 39, 41, 42, 45, 48, 50, 51, 52, 53, 55, 56, 58, 61, 62, 65, 67, 89, 91, 92, 95, 98, 102, 104
   156 'Sharknose' 18
   250 GT SWB 'Breadvan' 107
   312PB 6, 25-26, 27, 32, 35, 37, 41, 45, 46, 47, 48, 52, 56, 71, 100
   365 GTB/4 62
   365 P2 86, 87
   512 21
   Daytona GT 38
Ferrari, Enzo 10, 48
Fiat 10
Fletcher, Andrew 6, 45, 71, 83, 84, 85, 86, 87, 89, 91, 92
Fletcher, Henry 91, 92
Ford 29, 45
   Capri RS 2600 56, 62
   GT40 84
Formula 1 6, 8, 10, 13, 18, 21, 29, 33, 35, 36, 39, 41, 42, 47, 53, 57, 58, 61, 62, 68, 86, 87, 96, 98
Formula 3 39, 47
Fotiadis, Perikles 72, 74, 75, 79, 80
Francisci, Claudio 31
Galli, Nanni 18, 19, 21, 25, 29, 32, 34, 36, 37, 41, 42, 45, 46, 47, 48, 50, 51, 52, 53, 54, 61, 62, 103
Gauld, Graham 85, 91
Goodwood
   Festival of Speed 89, 91, 92
   Revival 107
Gosselin, 'Taf' 21
Grand Prix
   Angolan 84
   Austrian 53
   Belgian 10, 47
   Brazilian 39
   British 47
   Cremona 10
   Dutch 62
   French 10, 39, 52, 53
   German 10, 12, 39
   Italian 10, 53
   Monaco 10
   Nürburgring Oldtimer 100, 104
   South African 47
   Spanish 47
   Supercortemaggiore 14
   Turin 12
Gregg, Peter, 37, 41
Halusa, Lukas 103, 104, 107
Halusa, Martin 6, 100, 102, 103, 104, 107

Halusa, Niklas 103, 107
Hannen, Peter 87, 89
Haywood, Hurley 37, 41
Heinz, Dave 37, 41
Hezemans, Toine 6, 22, 24, 27, 32, 34, 36, 41, 48, 50, 52, 61, 94
Hill, Graham 57, 62
Hill, Phil 18
Hine, John 35, 56
Hobbs, David 45, 46
Hockenheim 33, 48
   Prix du Baden-Württemberg 48
Hulme, Nigel 89
Hutchinson, Jeff 32, 38, 48
Ickx, Jacky 35, 37, 41, 45, 46, 55
Imola 21, 48, 53, 91, 107
   500Kms 25, 67, 68
   Classic 96
   Coppa d'Oro Shell 48
International Championship for Makes 8
ISO Marlboro-Cosworth DFV 49
Jacobson, Laurence 85, 89
Jano, Vittorio 10, 14
Jarier, Jean-Pierre 63, 68
Jenkinson, Denis 22, 48
Joest, Reinhold 45, 55, 62
Johnson, Robert 37, 41
JW Automotive 31, 41
Kauhsen, Willi 48, 67, 68
Keranis 72, 74
Keyser, Michael 41, 52, 98
Killarney circuit 83, 87, 88
Kinnunen, Leo 48, 52
Kling, Karl 14
Knight, Mike 83, 84, 86, 87, 89
Kyalami 71, 86, 87, 89
   Nine-Hour 87
Lancia 48
   Beta Monte Carlo 98
   Fulvia 52
Larrousse, Gérard 35, 41, 56, 61
Lauda, Niki 18
'Iaveris' 76, 77, 81
Le Mans
   24 Hours 8, 10, 13, 14, 20, 21, 27, 31, 33, 38, 39, 41, 42, 57, 58, 61, 62, 65, 67, 68, 84, 104, 108
   Classic 96, 102, 107

Lennep, Gijs van 22, 25, 31, 33, 39, 48, 55, 56
Ligier JS2 61
Lola 35, 36, 41, 42, 59, 61, 62, 68, 77
   T70 86, 87, 89
   T212 39, 52
   T280 32, 38, 41, 42, 45, 46, 52, 56
Lola-Cosworth DFV 61
Lotus Europa 39, 48
Luraghi, Guiseppe 16, 18
Lyons, Pete 35, 38, 41
Maranello 18, 31, 51
Marelli, Giovanni 42, 75
Maris, Erik 96, 98
Marko, Dr Helmut 6, 31, 32, 35, 36, 37, 38, 39, 41, 42, 45, 46, 48, 50, 51, 52, 54, 55, 56, 57, 61, 62, 71, 76, 81, 91, 96, 98, 126
Markouizos, Tasos see 'Iaveris'
Martini International 25, 31, 33, 39, 53
Matra 58, 66, 67
   MS670 61, 62
Matra-Simca 61
   MS650 87, 89
McLaren 36, 47
   M7C 39
   M7D 53
   M8 48,
Meiners, Franco 6, 91, 92, 94, 95, 96, 98, 100, 102
Mercedes-Benz 8, 10, 12, 83
Merzario, Arturo 6, 45, 48, 50, 51, 52, 55, 56, 67, 68, 74, 91
Migault, Francois 46
Mille Miglia 8, 13, 14, 48, 57
Mini Cooper S 53, 80
Mirage 31, 61
   M6-Cosworth DFV 41, 42, 45, 55, 56
Monte Carlo Rally 35, 39
Montlhéry, Paris 1,000Kms 26
Monza 38, 49, 53, 74, 89, 107
   1,000Kms 45, 67, 68
Moschous, George (Giorgos) 6, 65, 72, 74, 75, 76, 77, 79, 80-81, 85
Moschous, Manolis 72, 74, 77, 80, 85
Moschous, Paul 72, 74, 80, 81
Motor Hellas 72, 75, 76, 79, 80, 81
Motor 57
Motor Sport 22, 42, 48, 87
Motoring News 25, 35, 36, 42, 45, 48, 52, 61

Mugello 16, 19, 53
Munari, Sandro 48, 50, 51, 52
Nissan 76, 81
Nürburgring 10, 16, 19, 19, 21, 27, 31, 33, 39, 66
   ADAC-1,000Kms-Rennen 54-56
Nuvolari, Tazio 8, 10, 12, 14, 48, 58
Österreichring 21, 25, 62
   1,000Kms 67
Pairetti, Carlos 35, 36
Panayote, Arvanitakis Denis 72, 74, 81
Parkes, Mike 62
Paul Ricard 27, 67, 96, 107
Pescarolo, Henri 22, 25, 27, 62, 68, 74
Peterson, Ronnie 27, 35, 37, 41, 46, 55, 56
Piccolo Circuit, Sicily 6
Piëch, Ferdinand 31, 33
Piper, David 83, 84, 85, 86, 87, 89, 92
Pirro, Emanuele 102, 107
Porsche 21, 24, 27, 29, 31, 33, 39, 55, 62, 67, 87, 95
   66 62
   907 33
   908 21, 22, 27, 31, 33, 45, 52, 61, 62
   908 LH 62
   908/02 46, 62
   908/03 24, 25, 31, 35, 62, 108
   910 41
   911 25, 33, 52
   911 S 37, 41, 52, 56
   914/6 41, 52
   917 18, 21, 22, 31, 33, 39, 42, 48, 61, 67, 87
   917/10 48
   917/30 33
Rattazzi, Gianluca 49, 102
Red Bull 6, 39, 96, 98
The Red Bulletin 50, 96
Redman, Brian 31, 35, 37, 46, 55, 56, 103
Regazzoni, Gianclaudio 'Clay' 25, 35, 36, 37, 45, 46, 53, 55, 56, 65
Revson, Peter 36, 37, 41, 42, 45, 46
Ricciardo, Daniel 6, 96, 98
Ritsona 79, 80
Road & Track 58,
Robinson, Brian 46
Rodríguez, Pedro 35, 42
Romeo, Nicola 10
Samways, Tim 49, 94, 95, 100, 102, 103, 104, 107, 108

Sanesi, Consalvo 14
Schenken, Tim 35, 37, 41, 46, 55, 56
Schmid, Dieter 52, 56
Sebring 12 Hours 16, 31, 33, 35, 38, 40-41, 42, 61
Severi, Gherardo 22, 27
Sicily 22, 25, 31, 51, 71, 92-98
Siffert, Jo 35
Silverstone 38, 85, 89, 103
   Classic 104
Smale, Glen 87
Smith, Robin 84, 85, 86
Sommer, Raymond 10, 14, 58
Spa-Francorchamps 45, 48, 65
   1000Kms 22
   Six Hours 107
Steckkönig, Günter 52, 56,
Stommelen, Rolf 8, 21, 25, 27, 32, 33, 34, 36, 37, 41, 42, 45, 46, 48, 49, 52, 54, 61, 62, 65, 67
Surtees 47
   TS9B 47
Targa Florio 6, 8, 10, 14, 16, 19, 22, 24, 25, 27, 33, 39, 42, 45, 48, 50, 52, 54, 61, 65, 67, 68, 71, 91, 98, 126
Tatoi circuit 74, 75, 76, 77, 80
Toro Rosso 39, 96
Tuckett, Willie 6, 22, 83, 84, 85, 86, 87, 89, 91, 92
Vaccarella, Nino 6, 19, 22, 24, 25, 27, 35, 36, 38, 41, 48, 50, 53, 61, 62, 98
Vallelunga 16, 47, 53
   6 Hours 67
Varzi, Achille 10, 14, 48
Viconopoulos, Chronis 80, 81
Voula hillclimb 76, 79, 80
Watkins Glen Six Hours 25, 27, 47, 62, 67, 68
Willi Kauhsen Racing Team (WKRT) 98
Wimille, Jean-Pierre 13
Wisell, Reine 36, 41
Zeccoli, Teodoro 16, 24, 25, 38, 67, 72, 75, 95